For David & Brenda,
With My Best Wishes!
Ken eakins

A Hill of Beans

WORTH FROM A BIBLICAL PERSPECTIVE

Gateway Seminary Library

j. kenneth eakins

Unless otherwise indicated, the Scripture quotations contained herein
are from the New Revised Standard Version Bible, copyright, 1989,
by the division of Christian Education of the
National Council of Churches of Christ in the U.S.A.

Copyright © 2005

All rights reserved.
No part of this book may be reproduced in any form
or by any means without permission in writing from the author.

ISBN 0-9662154-5-1

First Printing, 2005

Printed in the United States of America

This book is dedicated
With appreciation and affection
To the members of
The Agape Bible Class,
Tiburon Baptist Church

Contents

	Dedication	iii
	Acknowledgments	vii
	Preface	xi
1	Dollars and Sense	1
2	Education, Knowledge, and Wisdom	19
3	Fame and Acclaim	39
4	Power	57
5	I Just Want to Be Happy	75
6	A Name for a "Nobody"	93
7	In the Image of God	111
8	Living a Worthy Life	129

Acknowledgments

During the writing of this book, I have followed my usual practice of inviting others to participate in the process. Four persons, all members of the church to which I belong, read the entire manuscript, chapter by chapter, as it was being written. Let me introduce you to these wonderfully talented persons, whose insights and suggestions have been of tremendous help.

Jennifer Adams, a native of California, has been a public school teacher for twenty-one years—and she still loves teaching! Currently, she teaches math to first, fifth, sixth, seventh, and eighth graders, as well as California history and geography to fourth graders, and United States history and Geography to fifth graders. She and her husband, Bob, have a twelve-year old son, Zachary.

Barbara Dabney grew up in Alaska and she loves the outdoors—especially when it is cold! She enjoys working with infants, toddlers, and preschoolers at church, where she seeks to model God's love, mercy, grace, and goodness to children in their early formative years. Barbara's profession is librarianship, and for several years she was Director of Library Services at Golden Gate Baptist Seminary.

Jerry Good is a native of Iowa and is a graduate of the

University of Iowa Dental School. He spent three years on active duty in the United States Military. Following that, Jerry practiced dentistry in California for thirty-seven years. He is now enjoying retirement! He and his wife, Judy, have two grown sons, John and Jason, and two grandchildren.

Tom Jones is a native of Arkansas. He has an Ed. D. degree from Pepperdine University in Los Angeles. He is now serving as Vice President for Institutional Advancement at Golden Gate Baptist Seminary. Tom and his wife, Gail, have a twenty-two year old daughter, Sarah, and a seventeen-year old son, Matthew. Tom loves bluegrass music and is a great banjo player!

In addition to these four, I asked two other persons to read and comment on specific chapters. I treasure their expertise and their willingness to help with this project.

Martha Saul is a licensed Marriage and Family Therapist, with a large, active practice. She and I are members of the same church. Martha was kind enough to read chapter six and to share her wise insights and counsel with me. Many thanks, Martha!

Barry Stricker is my pastor at Tiburon Baptist Church. Formerly, he was professor of theology and Christian philosophy at Golden Gate Baptist Seminary. I asked Barry to read chapter seven. I am pleased that he concurs with the theology expressed there! Thanks for your help, Barry.

Also, I was delighted when Janet Reese volunteered to proofread the completed manuscript. Janet works as an Acquisitions/Serials Library Assistant at Golden Gate Baptist Seminary, and is also an adjunct faculty member in the area of Music History and Research. Thanks, Janet.

These seven persons make this a better book, but I claim all of its shortcomings. As the author, I had to make my own final decisions concerning content and its presentation. I hope that I have chosen well, but you, the reader, will have the final word!

I have also consulted a few other persons who helped track down various bits of information for my use, and I am grateful for their help. These include two of my daughters, Sheri Johnson and Nancy Kuykendall; also three of my friends, Judy Good, Dwight Honeycutt, and Elmer Meyer. Another friend, Gary Arbino, provided immense technical help with my computer and printer—especially on those occasions when they chose to be unfriendly!

For more than thirty years, I have had the joy of teaching the Agape Bible Class at Tiburon Baptist Church. The members have been very supportive and encouraging to me during the writing of this book. With great delight and appreciation, I dedicate this book to them.

Finally, this entire book has been written with the support of my beloved Marian. Although she has now been in heaven for more than fourteen years, she remains very close to me. Every idea and sentence has been subjected to her invisible scrutiny. More than once, I have made changes as a result of her presence. This is *our* book. We hope you will find it of interest—and *worth*.

Preface

"Do you think you will ever amount to a hill of beans?" That was a question I was once asked by an older brother when I was a child growing up in the Missouri Ozarks. On other occasions, friends assured me (hopefully in jest), that I *would* never amount to a hill of beans! Thus, the question of worth was thrust on me in early life. I am still probing its dimensions.

The colloquial American saying, "hill of beans," has been used widely since the mid-1800s. When the movie, *Casablanca*, was released in 1942, the expression was catapulted into greater prominence when Humphrey Bogart told Ingrid Bergman near the end of the film, "Ilsa, I'm no good at being noble, but it doesn't take much to see that the problems of three little people don't amount to a hill of beans in this crazy world."

"Hill of Beans" is a metaphor used to describe that which is of negligent and trifling value—that which has little or no worth. When used of things and activities, it often has limited significance. When applied to persons, however, very important issues always emerge—questions are posed that demand careful consideration and require adequate answers. These are issues and questions that this book addresses.

When my brother asked me that question over six decades ago, I had very little understanding of his query, and absolutely no basis for an appropriate answer. Now, after seventy-four birthdays and a life filled with varied experiences, observations, study, and reflection, I am bold enough to believe that I have gained some insight into what is worth a hill of beans—and what isn't.

Readers should note that I am a Christian and that this book is written from a Christian perspective. I have sought to expose all of my thoughts to the searchlight of Scripture. All biblical quotations are taken from the New Revised Standard Version unless otherwise noted. I have subjected my conclusions to the scrutiny of a panel of knowledgeable and respected Christian friends (see Acknowledgments). I believe, however, that all readers, regardless of their faith orientation, will find this book instructive and helpful.

Most of the people whom I know want to be successful, and they strive to achieve this in a variety of ways. When my children were younger, our family sometimes played a board game called *Careers*. The concept of the game is quite simple. Individual players choose their own "formula for success" made up of varying amounts of money, fame, and happiness. Each player decides what value to give each of these three components of success, and then engages in various careers and activities during the game that will garner the required number of points to achieve their goal. The first player to find "success" wins the game.

In real life, "winners" and "successful" individuals are generally considered to be persons of demonstrated *worth*. As in the game, they are often those who have become wealthy, or who have achieved fame and acclaim for various reasons. And we often assume that they have also found happiness. This can be, of course, a false assumption.

I suppose that nearly everyone does want to be a person of worth. What this really means, however, and how to attain that goal, is a puzzle for many. Distortions are common. Some persons have an exaggerated sense of their worth, while others struggle with feelings of personal failure and worthlessness. Both groups are cause for concern.

Not long ago, I sat in the snack area of a popular book and music store, enjoying good coffee and an excellent blueberry scone. I found myself doing a mental "worth evaluation" of the customers in the store. I watched them carefully and could hear fragments of their conversations. They all appeared to be well educated, affluent, and confident. I noticed that some of them drove away in expensive cars. They seemed to "have it made." Surely, using the common standards of today, these men and women were persons of worth.

Then, I noticed four men at a nearby table. Three of these were obviously mentally challenged, on an "outing" with an attendant. Their clothing was clean, but rather shabby. I watched them as they sat quietly, apparently enjoying their soft drinks. They seemed vulnerable, possible targets of ridicule. None of them would ever be able to read the books crowded onto nearby shelves, or drive a car, or own a home. In scales devised by society, they could well weigh in as persons of little worth—less perhaps, in the eyes of some, than a hill of beans. But both groups—those shopping for books and the quiet ones seated near me—cried out for further consideration and evaluation. Most of all, definition was needed.

What constitutes true worth? Who can give a definitive answer to that vexing question? Is there a yardstick available to measure the worth of persons and the product of their lives? If so, where can it be found? These are some of the questions that I invite you to consider carefully as you read the pages of *A Hill of Beans*.

You will find this book to be of greater value and interest if you enter into dialogue with what I have written. Reading should always be an active process. Respond to my observations and suggestions. Pose your own questions. Make written notes as you work through the book—to facilitate this, space has been provided for your use. I recommend that you also discuss these matters with friends.

Am *I* worth a hill of beans? Are *you* worth a hill of beans? I think that I now know the answer to these questions. Read on—and see what *you* think.

CHAPTER ONE

Dollars and Sense

"How much is John worth?" In most American contexts today, that question would probably anticipate an answer in terms of John's net worth measured in dollars. Money, and what it can buy, is a commonly used gauge for success—and worth. In fact, some would say that it provides our identity. I recently saw a television ad for a certain type of car that assures viewers, "You are what you drive."

There is, of course, nothing particularly new about this. From time immemorial, before money as such existed, the importance of persons has been measured in terms of possessions—land, houses, livestock, and the like. In our culture, there has tended to be special worth assigned to those persons who were born into poverty and who have been able to achieve prosperity and success, *a la* the many "rags to riches" stories written by the American author, Horatio Alger (1834-1899).

Attitudes toward money and wealth begin to be shaped early in life. As children, we naturally tend to accept the financial philosophy and practice of our parents. Later, however, under the influence of society, and conditioned by our own experiences, we may begin to modify our earlier feelings about the importance of wealth. The value that we attach to having money, and the decisions we make concerning its use, are very important factors in determining the type of person we will become.

All of us, therefore, need to give serious consideration to various aspects of wealth, and determine what these mean to us. Specifically, we would be wise to decide what role, if there is any, wealth can play in helping us to become persons of true worth. I wonder how much a hill of beans costs?

This chapter is not meant to be a guide to personal finances, at least not as that concept is commonly understood. I am not concerned here with financial planning in the usual sense, and will not write about budgets, banking, investments, trusts, wills, and the like. Rather, I want to think with you about larger issues that are involved in the question of the relationship between worth and wealth. I believe it will be helpful to look closely at three areas: acquiring wealth, the value of wealth, and the dangers of wealth. What makes good sense—and what doesn't?

Acquiring Wealth

Most of us learn early in life that money doesn't grow on trees. Since money gained through criminal activity does not deserve consideration in this book, and since few if any of us will find a treasure chest full of gold and jewels, or win a big lottery, it looks like there are only two remaining likely ways to acquire wealth—work and inheritance. And since inherited wealth was presumably accrued originally through the labor of some relative or friend, we draw the conclusion that life's necessities and luxuries must be obtained through work. As God said to Adam long ago,

"By the sweat of your brow shall you get bread to eat" (Genesis 3:19a, New Jewish Version).

Do you remember the first money that you actually earned? Don't include any allowance your parents may have given you, even though some of this may have been based on assigned chores. My first earned income came from picking wild blackberries and gooseberries and peddling them to my neighbors. I found that being a young "business man" was very exciting, and I quickly spent my small profit on comic books!

Later, I mowed lawns for some of those same neighbors, and also earned a few dollars doing janitorial tasks at school. My first "real" job, however, was working one summer, at age seventeen, as a bellhop in a hotel. What I learned there was more valuable than what I earned. I believe that there is real benefit to be gained from obtaining some work experience early in life.

There are many categories of work. To name a few, we often speak of "blue-collar" jobs and "white-collar" jobs. We think of work that primarily exercises the mind or that which calls mainly for muscle power. Then, there is work that requires special talent and skill, as in music, art, acting, and athletics. Also, money itself may be the "worker," with the stock market providing one example.

Although some jobs are worth more in terms of salary paid, it is perilous to automatically assume that this is any indication of the worth of the laborer. Menial, low-paying jobs are often held by persons of sterling character, and some persons who are paid large sums of money are vacuous, shallow fakes—or just plain scoundrels. The value of persons must never be judged by the size of their bank accounts. And none of us should allow our identity to be derived from our jobs (or the kind of car we drive!).

Regardless of how we earn our income, an important question is, "How much money do we need?" Certainly, we would hope for enough to provide for the basic necessities of life (such as shelter, food, clothing, and health care), some luxuries that enrich life, and money to save for a "rainy day" and retirement. And surely most of us would want to be able to give some away for the good of others.

A well-known phenomenon is that many persons always want more money than they already have no matter how rich they may be. There is a real sense in which the desire for money (and possessions) is an addiction. This often leads to the addict working unreasonably long hours, holding down more than one job, having excessive fear about becoming unemployed, and putting important relationships and personal health at great risk, all to gain more dollars. The acquisition of "wealth" can sometimes cost far too much—much more than it is worth.

Among those who seem particularly prone to this affliction are persons who experienced significant economic deprivation in early life. Many older persons today had their attitude toward money permanently shaped, not always in healthy ways, by the Great Depression of the 1930s. Others have grown up since then in homes where money was scarce and poverty was a cruel tyrant. In both groups, there are those who attach a degree of importance to the never-ceasing accumulation of wealth and possessions that does, indeed, have all the hallmarks of addiction.

I have known several such individuals and it is apparent that they have never gained a feeling of economic security despite the acquisition of significant monetary wealth. Expensive cars, large and luxurious homes, and all the "toys" that money can buy provide a "security blanket" against bleak memories of the past—and still there is no inner sense of real security. No one has truly escaped his or her past history of poverty and become fully free until their addiction to money has been overcome.

One way to help overcome this type of addiction is to seek opportunities to do some *pro bono* work, or to participate in some type of community volunteer activity. We need to find ways to donate freely a portion of our time and skills for the benefit of others, regardless of how wealthy or poor we may be.

I tell a story in my book *Becoming One* (the Afterword for the book was written by my daughter, Laurie) about a physician who rendered some emergency medical care to my wife, who was afflicted with cancer. He met us in his office on a Sunday afternoon and provided the needed care. Although we had insurance, he refused all payment. He said, "I don't have to make a buck out of everything." His words are worth remembering. "Making a living" and acquiring wealth involves more—much more—than the accumulation of dollars.

There are persons, especially some of the *nouveau riche*, who like to make an open display of their wealth. Perhaps they do this as much to assure themselves that they are persons of worth as they do to convince others. On the other hand, there are those who develop an excessively conservative attitude toward the use of their dollars. Reasonable frugality, abhorrence of waste, and cautious expenditures can sometimes degenerate into an ugly stinginess.

Although there are many exceptions—one should not paint with too broad of a brush—I have personally found that persons with limited financial means are often more generous with their money than folks with large amounts of money at their disposal. However, not wanting to be misunderstood, I have also encountered rich individuals who are very generous, and poor persons who are much more miserly than they need to be. The important question is not how much money any of us may have—the real question is what attitude we have toward our financial resources and its proper use.

As noted previously, there are many different kinds of work. If we have any choice in the matter, I believe most of us would certainly choose a job that brings personal satisfaction. It is not pleasant to spend years toiling at work that one dislikes—and it is difficult to feel good about one's self in those circumstances. Also, I would hope that we would avoid types of employment that seek to mislead, exploit, and even cause injury to others. Such pursuits, often the result of corporate and personal greed, may be "profitable," but no amount of dollars can ever justify the harm done. What value can there be in money obtained in dishonorable (even if legal) ways? For that matter, how valuable is wealth?

The Value of Wealth

Wealth is a word full of content, but in this chapter we will continue to focus on it in the limited meaning of money and what money can buy. Other dimensions will be explored later. So—of what value are dollars?

All of us have heard these common maxims: "You can't buy happiness," "The best things in life are free," and "You can't take it with you." Probably few persons would argue with the wisdom contained in the first two of these sayings (they make a lot of sense), and certainly no one can doubt the third! Two biblical writers make that point quite well. "Naked I came from my mother's womb, and naked I will depart" (Job 1:21a, New International Version). "For we brought nothing into the world, and we cannot take anything out of the world" (1 Timothy 6:7, Revised Standard Version).

And so again the important question, do dollars have any significant value? The answer, of course, is "Yes." No intelligent, realistic person can deny the value and importance of money. Obviously, it provides a convenient medium of exchange. Long ago, before coined money came into existence and use in the seventh century B.C., transfer of goods from one person to another could be quite cumbersome. The barter system, where persons traded labor and goods with one another for desired items, was often complicated and far from satisfactory in many cases.

Also, the practice of using a balance scale where an amount of precious metal, usually silver, was weighed against some commodity, such as grain, fruit, or vegetables, was subject to a good bit of abuse and fraud. Because there was no standardization of weights and measures, and with an absence of any system to regulate the accuracy of scales, the customer was often cheated by unscrupulous merchants (for an interesting picture of this, see Amos 8:4-6 in the Old Testament).

Coins (and later paper money) brought some much-needed order into business transactions of all sorts. Coins were more, however, than just a valuable medium of exchange. They were also the "newspapers" of the ancient world, in a time when none of the common forms of media known today existed. As they circulated widely, their artwork and inscriptions carried such news as the birth of a nation, the installation of a new ruler, an important military victory, and a host of other newsworthy items. Today, money—especially coins—is still used at times to celebrate and commemorate significant events. By the way, allow the archaeologist in me to observe that the counterfeiting of money is not just a modern problem—it was widely practiced in ancient times.

Beyond simply making it *easier* to transact business, money has become *necessary* to obtain most of the goods and services required to provide life's basic necessities. If you take a lamb or a basket of fruit to a department store at the Mall to trade for clothing, I doubt if you will be successful. How would they ring that up on the cash register?! (Many people now shun the use of cash for most purchases, including small ones, and pay with checks, credit cards, or debit cards. Several years ago one of my daughters worked in a coffee shop. Just for fun, she placed a sign at the cash register saying that those paying in cash should be prepared to show two forms of ID. The humorous thing is that some customers took it seriously!)

In addition to the requirements of individuals, the larger community (local, state, and national) also has needs. We fund these with our tax dollars—schools, for example, and police and fire protection, roads, public health departments, national defense, and a long list of other valuable and necessary services. Unfortunately, in times of financial distress some communities are too quick to reduce funding to some vulnerable but very important entities such as parks and libraries.

Money is also valuable in that it makes it possible for us to more easily acquire and enjoy some things that enrich our life. Certainly everyone should be able to have at least a few luxuries, including opportunities for travel, if desired. Our tastes will vary greatly (and many persons have difficulty differentiating between luxuries and necessities).

Readers of my book *Long Shadows* might remember

that I appreciate greatly the mystery stories written by Agatha Christie. When one of her sleuths, Miss Jane Marple, an elderly spinster with limited financial means, realized that she might receive a significant amount of unexpected money, she first thought of several charities to which she wanted to make contributions. But she also dreamed of a few luxuries that she would certainly enjoy—candied chestnuts, an occasional partridge for dinner, and the opportunity to go to the opera once in a while (*Nemesis*, chapter two). I suspect many of us would have much more extravagant ideas! Miss Marple, however, was a very smart lady, full of wisdom and much common sense.

A real benefit of dollars and other tokens of wealth is that they make it easier for us to determine rather exactly the amount of our monetary assets. With this information we are able to calculate with some precision what we can afford to buy—and what we cannot! With careful planning, our bills can be paid on time and saving for future expenses can be undertaken in an orderly fashion. We can know the satisfaction of being in control over our assets, whether they are great or small. Surprises over unexpected demands on our budget can be met with less shock, confusion, and desperation.

Another important value of having wealth is that it permits us the opportunity to share with others. This is something that all of us should *want* to do. However, giving a portion of our financial resources away does call for wisdom and discretion. This is especially true for any of us who may have a sizeable fortune. Expert financial guidance will probably be necessary in such cases.

But whether our own monetary assets are modest or great, appropriate ways should be found to share these. The only known antidote to the ugly and mortal sin of selfishness is generosity and liberality in sharing all of our resources, including our money, with other persons. The other side of the coin is that we will want to be gracious receivers if we should ever be the recipients of someone else's generosity.

Hoarded dollars, held in tightfisted fashion, can only bring one a twisted, distorted sense of satisfaction and worth. Giving freely to others—individuals, suitable causes, and worthy charities—brings great joy and blessing to the donors as well as to the recipients. I firmly believe that generosity in the use of our financial resources is an *essential* component of joy. It just makes good sense!

There is deep wisdom in the biblical concept of giving at least a tithe (ten percent) of one's income back to God to be used to help others. Many persons are in a position to give more than a tithe—and it is a joyous experience to do so. This is true, however, only if we give willingly. As the Apostle Paul said, "Each one must do as he has made up his mind, not reluctantly or under compulsion, for God loves a cheerful giver" (2 Corinthians 9:7, Revised Standard Version).

One of my favorite authors, loved by many throughout the world, is C. S. Lewis. Although not a poor man, he chose to live a very simple lifestyle in modest surroundings. An enormous monetary profit could have been his, derived from the sale of his numerous and very popular books. However, Lewis elected to give away most of the income earned from his writings and live on his salary as a professor. Lewis was a Christian who was quite aware of the value of money, but he was also keenly alert to the perils of wealth. Let us now turn to a consideration of those dangers.

The Dangers of Wealth

Do you remember the Greek myth about Midas, king of Phrygia? Let remind you of this fascinating story. The god Dionysus (Bacchus), in return for help that Midas had given his old teacher, Silenus, offered to grant him one wish. Midas requested that everything he touched would turn into gold. With reluctance, Dionysus granted his request—and Midas very quickly found himself in serious trouble. All of his food, even that which his servants tried to feed him, turned into gold! In some versions of the story, his young daughter, Zoe, became a victim.

In desperation, Midas prayed to Dionysus for help. The god told him to bathe in the river Pactolus and his now unwelcome power would be removed. Midas obeyed and he returned to his usual state, and water that he carried from the river to pour on his daughter restored her to life. Midas found out the hard way that gold could be a curse! This, of course, is only an old myth. Let's return to the real world and listen carefully to these words of Jesus.

"Truly, I say to you, it will be hard for a rich man to enter the kingdom of heaven. Again, I tell you, it is easier for a camel to go through the eye of a needle than for a rich man to enter the kingdom of God" (Matthew 19:23-24, Revised Standard Version). When Jesus spoke these emphatic words to his disciples, they were, understandably, astonished! Jesus went on to say that with the help of God even that which seems impossible can actually happen. But we all need to take seriously his warning that riches can be a serious impediment to entry into God's kingdom.

Jesus was born into an economically poor family. When he was forty days old, his parents brought him to the Temple in Jerusalem to be dedicated (Luke 2:22-24).

The Jewish Law specified that two sacrifices were to be offered on such occasions—one lamb a year old and one young pigeon or turtledove. However, the Law also stated that if a family could not afford a lamb, then two birds were acceptable (Leviticus 12:6-8). Joseph and Mary brought two birds!

Joseph was a small-town carpenter (Matthew 13:55), and Jesus also engaged in this trade (Mark 6:3) until he began his public ministry when he was about thirty years old. Jesus—the One through whom all things were made (John 1:3) and the Lord of the cosmos—never earned any large sums of money on earth, but he certainly observed the corrupting influence that wealth had on many people.

The Apostle Paul was also aware of how dangerous the quest for wealth could become. He wrote these insightful and stark words to his younger colleague, Timothy: "For the love of money is a root of all sorts of evil" (1 Timothy 6:10a, New American Standard Bible). Please notice that Paul said it is the *love* of money—not money itself—that is the culprit. Let's look at some of the ways that this misguided love is dangerous and even deadly.

The love of money can easily become an addiction, as noted earlier. Soon a person may find himself or herself focusing more and more on the pursuit of dollars. Many good and enjoyable facets of life (such as books, concerts, gardening, travel, vacations—everyone can add to this list) are slowly crowded out and eliminated by relentless pressure from the constricting vice of one's job(s). Particularly vulnerable, as previously mentioned, are relationships with family members and friends. Also placed at great risk is one's own physical, emotional, mental, and spiritual health.

An inordinate desire for money can also tempt one to engage in practices that are unethical, immoral, or even downright illegal. I'm afraid that the popular phrase, "It is only business," often seeks to conceal a multitude of evils. The conscience of one who participates in such activities can easily become seared and hardened to the point where the ability to distinguish between right and wrong becomes difficult or impossible.

Greed to acquire money—by whatever means necessary—can lead the one who is "successful" to a pair of the greatest evils of all—pride and selfishness. How easy it is to become excessively proud of one's possessions! How often this is accompanied by an ugly selfishness! And now we are in the clutches of real evil. Movement from this domain of evil to the realm of God's kingdom is very difficult indeed—as hard as it is for a camel to go through the eye of a needle!

I suggest that you take time to read a parable of Jesus about a rich man, as told in Luke 12:13-21. Jesus prefaces this parable with these words, "A man's life does not consist in the abundance of his possessions" (Verse 15b. This and the following two quotations from the parable are from the Revised Standard Version).

The man in this parable did not share the view of Jesus about possession. His land was productive and his barns were filled to overflowing. His solution was to tear them down and build larger ones in which to store his grain and other goods. He was content with his life and said to himself, "Soul, you have ample goods laid up for many years; take your ease, eat, drink, be merry" (Verse 19). God's response, found in verse 20, was to ask the man, "Fool! This night your soul is required of you; and the things you have prepared, whose will they be?"

If you read this parable closely, it becomes apparent that this was a proud man and a very selfish one. As he reflected on his seemingly favored status, he used the personal pronoun "I" six times. Not once did he refer to anyone else or consult with another person. He was a self-sufficient, wealthy man. But in reality, he didn't "own" anything—and certainly not his soul. It doesn't look like his wealth was worth much, does it?

I have always found C. S. Lewis' book, *The Screwtape Letters*, interesting and instructive. This book records counsel and directions given by Screwtape, a senior devil, to his nephew, Wormwood, a junior devil. At one point, Screwtape tells Wormwood that he should urge a human under his "care" to seek possessions. "The sense of ownership in general is always to be encouraged. The humans are always putting up claims to ownership which sound equally funny in Heaven and Hell." But, as Screwtape notes, ultimately either Satan or God "will say 'mine' of each thing that exists, and especially of each man" (Chapter 21). I am afraid it was Satan who claimed the rich man in the parable we have been studying. (For another biblical story about the deadly consequences of loving money, I suggest that you read the parable of the rich man and Lazarus in Luke 16:19-31.)

The love of money is indeed the source of all sorts of evil and everyone upon whom the shadow falls is hurt—sometimes eternally. We have been thinking about rich persons, but we need to remember that one does not have to be wealthy to love money. Often persons of modest means are seriously ill with this malady. It is sad that this love will cause some people who have few treasures on earth to also have none in heaven.

Love of money certainly has the power to lead us into evil practices as we attempt to acquire wealth, and also in our use of the financial assets we possess. Such love certainly has a deadly way of making us blind and deaf to the presence and voice of God. Just before Jesus spoke to his disciples about how difficult it is for a rich person to enter the kingdom of God, he had been in conversation with a young man who wanted to know how to obtain eternal life. The man was quite moral and claimed to have carefully kept the Law, but he sensed something lacking in his life.

Jesus quickly diagnosed the man's problem and offered a solution. He advised the man to sell his possessions, give to the poor, and become a disciple of Jesus. This was the response: "When the young man heard this he went away sorrowful; for he had great possessions" (Matthew 19:22, Revised Standard Version). And Jesus sadly thought about a camel and the eye of a needle!

Many, many times during my lifetime I have observed persons blinded to the claims of God on their life by the lure of money and the glitter of possessions. God is ignored, or given second place—which is, of course, to give him no legitimate place at all. Such persons have no treasure in heaven and, sooner or later, they will have none on earth. Everything is lost.

Jesus had a practice of asking penetrating questions. A good example is found in Matthew 16:26, which I translate this way: "What benefit will it be for a person if he gains the whole world, and in the process forfeits his soul? Or, what is a person willing to give in exchange for his soul?" The folly of living such an ill-spent life is captured in these words of an old Gospel song by Anna Olander: "If I gained the world, but not the Savior, Were my life worth living for a day?" The obvious answer is an emphatic "No"!

In another parable (see Matthew 13:45-46), Jesus tells a story to illustrate the transcendent worth of the kingdom of Heaven. A merchant was seeking fine pearls and when he found one of unsurpassed value, he sold all that he had and bought that pearl—it just made sense! That one pearl was worth much more than all the others combined. Life with God on earth, and eternal fellowship in his presence, is the greatest treasure any of us can ever possess. We are very foolish if we let the love of money get in the way—and we are poor beyond description.

The Sum of the Matter

Perhaps it is time for an audit. Let's draw a few conclusions about the matter of wealth and worth. My conviction is that only God can truly assess the worth of any human being. So, is wealth evidence that God has found a person worthy? Through the centuries some have thought so. I believe it is beyond dispute that many people today do measure their worth as individuals by their financial assets. This is a mistaken idea that cannot be substantiated or documented in any way by Scripture. There is no direct correlation between worth as a human being and financial wealth. A sensible examination of the biblical evidence leads to this conclusion.

This is also the conclusion that my close observation of persons on the playing field of life has led me to accept. Both as a Christian minister and as a physician, I have had the opportunity to be included in meaningful and substantial ways in the lives of persons representing all parts of the financial spectrum. Right now, my thoughts stray to an afternoon long ago when I made a house call to see one of my patients, a little girl whose parents were desperately poor. When I left their small home, I drove directly to the large residence of a boy who was seriously ill. His parents were extremely wealthy.

I knew both of these families well enough to feel confident that they were all persons of authentic worth. Many times I have had similar experiences—and I have never been able to see any causal relationship between the absence or presence of wealth and the true worth of any individual.

I suggest that you take a dollar from your wallet or purse just now and hold it in your hands. Look at it carefully and thoughtfully. That dollar itself is totally neutral—it cannot make you or me a better person or a worse person. Our attitude toward money and the way we use money can, however, have a profound impact on our quality of life, and can reveal to a significant extent the kind of person we really are. Let's resolve to make that dollar bill—and all the others we have and will have—our servant and not our master. Jesus clearly taught that we are not able to serve both God and money (Matthew 6:24).

If you and I are wealthy, we can employ our monetary resources in worthy ways to enrich our lives and the lives of others. Much good can be accomplished through the careful use of our financial resources. If we are poor, we must not think that this is proof that we are of no value . . . personal worth and value are not gained through the accumulation of wealth. It might also be well to acknowledge that there is much about wealth that is relative—not absolute. Probably most of us who are poor and live in the United States would be considered wealthy by a large number of persons living elsewhere.

Money, possessions, and wealth—these are neither good nor bad, but they have the potential of becoming either a curse or a blessing. And the love of money, as we have seen, can be exceedingly dangerous. We need to ask God to help us remove that type of love from our life and replace it with a love that brings joy and peace (Galatians 5:22-23).

Well, if money and possessions cannot make us worth more than a hill of beans, perhaps education can. Is success in our pursuit of worth a matter of obtaining knowledge? A lot of people seem to think so. Let's now move on to a consideration of that possibility.

CHAPTER TWO

Education, Knowledge and Wisdom

Schools have been around for a very long time—longer than the ones your grandparents might have attended and probably have told you stories about! As early as 2500 B.C. schools had become an important part of the flourishing civilization developed by the Sumerians in southern Mesopotamia (now part of Iraq). At first these schools were primarily for teaching reading and writing; soon, however, the curriculum expanded to include a broad range of subjects.

These ancient Sumerian schools were for the sons of the wealthy, and their purpose was to educate boys for work in temples and government offices. School days were long (from sunrise to sunset, with only six days off each month) and discipline was *very* strict. For some interesting reading, I highly recommend *History Begins at Sumer* by Samuel Noah Kramer. The title of the first chapter is "The First Schools." Chapter two is called "The First Case of 'Apple Polishing.'" The entire book is fascinating.

Through the centuries, nations came to recognize the importance of an educated citizenry, both men and women. Public schools were founded, and these were funded, not always adequately, by tax money. Attendance requirements for children were established, and teachers were required to have appropriate education and credentials.

After their years of childhood and youth, numerous persons aspired to education beyond that mandated for them by the state. Dreams of attending college were often realized. Many believed that the value of a good education was worth almost any amount of effort and sacrifice. Today, most people probably continue to feel this way, even though the financial cost of attending college and graduate school continues to increase.

I am one of those who have a profound appreciation for schools, teachers, and the importance of education. Most of my life to this point has been spent as a student or a professor in some type of formal schooling. If I chose to do so (which I don't), I could list five earned degrees after my name, two of them doctorates. Doesn't this indicate conclusively that I am a person of worth? Well-l-l—perhaps the relationship between education and worth needs to be considered more thoroughly!

The Value of Education

Many people consider the importance of education from a strictly pragmatic point of view. The idea, usually correct, seems to be: "Education will help me find a better job." And for most, "better" means a higher-paying job, perhaps in business or one of the professions. In the game "Careers," referred to in the Preface, completing college automatically increases the amount of salary each player receives as he or she passes "Payday" each trip around the board. In real life, studies have documented that persons with a college degree usually do have higher lifetime earnings than those without a college education.

There are, however, a variety of things to keep in mind. I find it ironic that teachers, upon whom so much depends, have traditionally not been paid very well—a pattern already established in ancient Sumer. This is a shortsightedness of society that needs correction. But it is difficult. Several years after I graduated from high school, when I was a student in medical school, I wrote a letter that was published in my hometown newspaper. I urged the citizens to support a tax increase that was badly needed to provide more adequate funding for the schools that had been so vitally important in my own early education—the initiative failed. But the quest to provide quality public education must never be abandoned. Private schools and home schooling, while of value to some, cannot provide for the educational needs of the vast majority of students. It is vital that we support our public schools, including colleges and universities.

We must acknowledge, however, that many persons are able to secure a good financial income with little or no higher education, or with training obtained in vocational schools and apprenticeships. And some—professional athletes immediately come to mind—often earn huge salaries despite minimal formal education in many cases. The truth remains, however, that the most common road out of poverty and perhaps to affluence goes through our schools.

Since I believe I have already established, in chapter one, the futility of seeking worth through money, let's not linger here any longer. I am very glad that many people visualize the value of education in ways that do not cause $ $ signs to dance in their eyes. What *does* motivate these persons to become educated?

Well, for one thing, there are those who desire education because they hope it will bring them increased respect, honor, and even prestige. Up to a point, this can be a valid and wholesome reason for going to school. Individuals and their families can have legitimate pleasure and pride over success in the academic arena, and self-confidence is often strengthened. But distortions of these worthy benefits can occur.

One aspect of education that has disturbed me for a long time is the tendency of some persons with advanced academic degrees to feel that they are superior to other persons. Society as a whole sometimes seems to support this unfortunate myth. This attitude is often very subtle, but the result can be an unjustified pride, and can lead to an unhealthy feeling about persons with less education, or those with training of a vocational nature.

I believe that I have credentials that allow me to comment on this issue. I worked very hard to obtain my education, and I value it highly. Because of my schooling, many important and worthwhile doors have been opened for me to enter. However, I have *never* felt that my degrees make me a better person than anyone else—*it just isn't so.* Furthermore, what I know to be true of myself, I also believe to be true of all other persons I have known with advanced degrees. There always seem to be a few, however, who lack insight into their own true status.

To illustrate, some persons tend to overly enjoy being called by special titles, such as "doctor," and they may take an unseemly delight in displaying their degrees and other tokens of their achievements. They remind me of the words of Jesus who cautioned his disciples *not* to be like some religious leaders at that time who loved "to be greeted with respect in the market place and to have people call them 'Teacher'" (Matthew 23:7, Today's English Version).

Among these folks are some who probably harbor secret doubts about their own inner merit and who are out to document for themselves that they really are worth something—that they have more value than a hill of beans! Sometimes they are able to satisfy themselves that this is so, but most often they find that education has not given them the sense of worth that they so earnestly desire. Maybe yet another degree will help?? Probably not.

Apart from an opportunity to earn more money, or to gain respect and honor, there are other reasons numerous people desire a good education. For instance, I have had the good fortune of knowing *many* men and women who have worked hard to obtain the knowledge and skills that equip them to be of service to others. The hope of helping others has been their primary motivation for pursuing education. These persons are often found among health-care providers, teachers, and staff members of churches. You, of course, can think of other categories of persons of this type. May their numbers increase!

As I wrote the words of the preceding paragraph, I was lingering over a cup of coffee in the Food Court area of a local Mall (not the place I refer to in the Preface, although the stories may sound a little similar). Just as I was preparing to leave, a pleasant looking young man with three mentally challenged men in his care came in and they sat at the table next to mine. As I left, I stopped and said hello to the group and thanked the leader for the worthwhile service he was providing. He was pleased, and remarked that his work was very rewarding—I am quite sure he was not talking about money.

There are also those who want a good education

because they believe it will provide a key to unlock certain treasures, past and present, and usher them into a fuller, happier, and more satisfying life. For me, this has always been a good reason to engage in learning experiences, both formal and informal.

Education can aid us to discover the joy of great literature, to appreciate music and art, and to experience the excitement of remarkable advances in science. It can also help us recognize our debt to the past and our continuity with those who have gone before, and to better plan for the future. And it should provide us direction and encouragement to become life-long learners. This is *very* important. While I was revising portions of this chapter, I received a card from a woman living in Oklahoma whom I do not know. She wrote to tell me that she had enjoyed reading one of my articles in the Holman Bible Dictionary. I receive such letters fairly often from persons responding to various things that I have written, and I am always pleased to hear from them. This particular letter, however, was extra special. Why? Because the woman who wrote is ninety-one years old!

I am delighted that this person is still reading articles in a Bible Dictionary! She is a good model to remind all of us of the importance of continuing to learn throughout our life. We should all attempt to be aware of what is happening today, including the remarkable advances in knowledge and technology. There is always more to learn from the *past and the present*—and it can be a lot of fun! To become intellectually stagnant is very dangerous at any age and in any time, and certainly this is true today.

Hopefully, we can learn to benefit from modern technology without becoming its captive. We should also seek to be more discriminating in our response to the onslaught of advertising and merchandizing that threatens to inundate us. During my first year in college, I enrolled in an English course that included an extremely helpful short unit on Propaganda.

Now, more than fifty years later, I can recognize those old familiar and misleading devices and gimmicks still being used by politicians in their speeches and interviews, or proclaimed in advertisements on the media for various products, or displayed in signs by some merchants—and I am not an easy target. I do not fall for smooth schemes and I am not frightened by scare-tactics. I am sorry, however, for the large amount of deception that we all encounter.

I am convinced that education is important and that it is worth obtaining. "Worth obtaining"—but does it make us persons of worth? That is the question that we continue to probe. There are some definite limits—even dangers—to be aware of as we seek to become truly educated persons.

The Limits of Education

The pursuit of education can be a frustrating and even risky matter. I have observed several hazards and mistakes that engulf many persons in the educational process. One of the most common of these is working for grades (and degrees) rather than focusing on learning. Pressure on a student, from the inside and outside, to obtain good grades can be immense. This can drain away the joy that should be part of schooling and can actually interfere with true learning. Unhealthy patterns of competition often develop, and cheating becomes commonplace.

Let me speak frankly about the matter of cheating. This is not just a harmless practice. While it might garner the cheater an "A" (or an "F"!) on some occasions, cheating clearly impedes learning. It *never* leads to individual integrity and certainly not to personal worth. Cheating is never justified—it is just plain wrong. I doubt if this bad and widespread practice can ever be completely eliminated from our schools, but attempts can be made to determine its motivation, expose its harmful nature, and reduce opportunities for it to occur.

To be successful, this will require the combined and coordinated effort of teachers, students, maybe counselors, and the parents of pre-adult students. The main focus should be on education and prevention. Attempts to reduce this plague are worth trying. I rather suspect that the "successful" cheater in school will continue the practice in other ways later on—such as cheating on resumes, expense accounts, tax reports, and the like. It can become a way of life—but this is most definitely not a road that leads to worth.

"Good grades" and "good education" are often not equivalent terms. Some of the smartest, most intelligent, and happiest persons whom I know were not "straight A" students during their formal schooling—but they still obtained an excellent education. Letter grades are—at best—an inexact measure of achievement and intelligence, and certainly are not designed to be indicators of personal worth.

In worst-case scenarios, it is not rare for students who are overly intent on achieving nothing but top grades to sacrifice wholesome interpersonal relationships, develop anxiety disorders and depression, and even resort to suicide. From their point of view, the pressures of school are just too great to bear. Initial hope and enthusiasm ends in disaster. No grade or degree can ever be worth such cost.

I have told elsewhere (in chapter two of *Less Than a Mile*) about the most satisfying portion of my own long educational journey—my four years in medical school. Those years, exceedingly difficult in a lot of ways, held many joys and delights. One of the things I liked most was that I never learned my final grade in any course I had taken until midway through my senior year. The emphasis was always on learning and not on grades—now isn't that a radical idea?! We students were free to learn, and not held in slavery by report cards. It was wonderful! (Of course I had *some* idea of how I was doing, and had I been failing, or not making satisfactory progress, I would have been informed of that *very quickly*!)

There are also those students who engage in higher education not because they want to, but because others—perhaps parents—more or less demand it. This places real strictures on the whole learning process and seriously limits its value. Not *everyone* wants or needs to go to college (but those who wish to should have the opportunity). And on a few occasions, I have counseled a student to seriously consider *not* enrolling in Ph.D. studies, because the sacrifice for him or her, and perhaps others, would likely be too great and the benefit too little. Just because you and I *can* do something does not mean that it is necessarily *worth* doing.

Another deficiency of education, in my opinion, is that over the last century it has become progressively more narrow and specialized. I have always admired "Renaissance" men and women—persons who have many interests and who have knowledge and at least some degree of understanding in several different fields of learning. No one, of course, can be a specialist in everything. Our world has now become much too complex for that. But I question whether persons are truly "educated" if their interests and abilities are totally focused on only one small subject or skill, even though they may display amazing brilliance in that area.

If removed from their narrow place of interest and expertise, these individuals often tend to be very naïve and gullible. And if they make endorsements and pronouncements about things that they actually know little or nothing about (a very common propaganda device) they can be misleading and even dangerous. Even though their achievements, honors, and reputations may be justifiably great, their opinions are worth very little when they are outside their small field of learning.

As we continue to consider the limits of education, the question of wisdom comes to mind. Although they are by no means mutually exclusive, education and wisdom are not the same. One can be educated and not possess wisdom; one can be wise and have little or no formal education. I have met some people (and I suspect you have also) who have spent many years in school and have accumulated some academic degrees along the way, but who seem to be rather foolish. These are often persons who have learned a lot of "facts," but who have never learned what these mean. They have learned "information," but not how to reason and think—and that is poor education.

Although wisdom is not easy to define, it is generally agreed that a wise person is adept at discerning between that which is actually true and that which is false. He or she also has the ability to know what is truly important and what isn't—what has genuine worth, and that which isn't worth a hill of beans. Wise persons can distinguish between the permanent and the ephemeral, and they know how to employ all they have learned in wholesome and productive ways. Such persons usually also demonstrate what is commonly called "common sense."

Formal schooling can enhance all of these attributes and qualities of wisdom, but has little success in producing them. (I doubt if a college course called "Common Sense 101" would be very helpful, but it might be worth trying!) Sometimes we are assured that, regardless of our amount of formal education, we will become wiser as we grow older. That does seem to happen often, but, on the other hand, you and I likely know at least a few rather foolish old men and women. I sure hope that we are not meeting them in the mirror!

Schools, education, knowledge, and wisdom—do these establish and mark the path, or at least one of the paths, to authentic worth? Can I become smart enough and clever enough to prove to myself and to the world that I really do have personal value? How intelligent do I have to be for this to happen, and who is qualified to determine when I have been successful? What if circumstances beyond my control deny me the opportunity to walk this path? Am I therefore doomed to worthlessness, or is there still hope? I believe we should now turn to the Bible for some help in answering these perplexing questions.

Guidance From Scripture

Does the Bible really have anything important to say to us about knowledge and wisdom? Yes, quite a lot. We would be very foolish to ignore and neglect what Scripture teaches. Let's consider it required reading. We will begin our examination at an early, critical moment in the history of humankind. You would do well to have a Bible close at hand for ready reference.

The first recorded attempt of human beings to acquire knowledge had a tragic ending. You are perhaps familiar with the story. In the second chapter of Genesis, we are told that God placed Adam and Eve, the couple he had created, in a beautiful garden. In the midst of the garden was an attractive symbolic tree—the Tree of Knowledge of Good and Evil. (I will discuss the nature of this tree further in chapter seven.) The couple was forbidden to eat the fruit of the tree that represented *all* knowledge because God knew that it would harm them.

The tree, however, was very pleasant to look at, and Adam and Eve were sure that its fruit would be tasty and nourishing. They also thought it would make them knowledgeable and wise—like God himself. Believing that they knew better than God what was in their best interests, they yielded to the lure of the temptation set before them by a skillful and evil Master Propagandist (see chapter three of Genesis).

But in the realm of knowledge, God had set a barrier between himself and all human life—and the first pursuit of forbidden knowledge ended in unspeakable tragedy. The couple was expelled from their lovely home, and access to another tree in the Garden, the Tree of Life, was denied them. Spiritual death had occurred and later the foolish pair would experience physical death. Since then, we have all followed in their ill-fated steps, making the same mistakes and suffering the same consequences.

When we begin to investigate the mistake of Adam and Eve, what emerges first is the nature of their motivation for desiring knowledge. They were driven by unrealistic ambition and undue pride. They wanted to be like God, to be omniscient and in full charge of their own destiny. But as human beings (which is what they were created to be), those desires were foolish, unreachable, and dangerous. God tells us, "For as the heavens are higher than the earth, so are my ways higher than your ways and my thoughts than your thoughts" (Isaiah 55:9).

Adam and Eve also chose to disobey the clear command of God (and all of us have followed their example). To obtain knowledge which they felt would be helpful and rewarding, they went their own way—not heeding the instruction of the Lord and ignoring his urgent warning. And God gives all of us this caution: "There is a way that seems right to a person, but its end is the way to death" (Proverbs 14:12).

Obviously, Adam and Eve were not very wise. Can you and I hope to gain wisdom and cease repeating the same old mistakes over and over again? Where is wisdom found? The ancient Hebrews pondered this question and they reached some interesting conclusions. Chapter 28 of the book of Job is a beautiful and thoughtful treatise on wisdom and it contains some helpful guidance for us. If possible, I encourage you to read through it right now.

As this chapter says, miners can probe deep into the earth and find silver, gold, iron, and copper. Likewise, you and I might be able to acquire some natural, earthly wisdom through our own effort and experience. But no human being, left to his or her own ingenuity, can ever find the way to *true* wisdom. Only God knows it source—hear this conclusion: "Listen! Awe and respect for the Lord—that is wisdom. And turning away from evil is understanding" (Job 28:28, My translation).

God is the *only* source of true wisdom. The good news is that he wants to share it with us. As we read in James 1:5 in the New Testament, "If any of you is lacking in wisdom, ask God, who gives to all generously and ungrudgingly, and it will be given you." James cautions us, however, that our request must be made with faith and without doubts. But there are other dimensions to this matter—consider the following story.

Solomon, a king of ancient Israel, is a glaring exception to the general rule that people tend to grow wiser as they age. He came to the throne as a teenager, and he felt grossly inadequate for the task before him. God came to Solomon in a dream and asked what he could give the new king. Solomon's reply was commendable: "Give your servant therefore an understanding mind to govern your people, able to discern between good and evil" (1 Kings 3:9). And we are told that, "God gave Solomon very great wisdom, discernment, and breadth of understanding . . ." (1 Kings 4:29).

Thus Solomon got off to a noble start in his reign. His reputation for being a wise king spread far and wide, and people came from great distances to see this remarkable monarch and to hear his words of wisdom. We are told that he composed three thousand proverbs (1 Kings 4:32). (The biblical book of Proverbs contains material collected under the name of Solomon, but it is unlikely that he is the actual author of many of these particular proverbs.) Thus, all began well for the new king—but all did not end well. This wise man in time came to be numbered among the most foolish!

A study of his record reveals that he did not formulate and exercise sound governmental policy. His personal life fell into shambles. He married many foreign women, and we are told that eventually he had seven hundred wives and three hundred concubines (1 Kings 11:3). Most devastating of all, he began to worship numerous gods. As a frustrated parent might say to a disobedient child, "You *know* better than that," so we would like to say those same words to Solomon, the wisest of men. And he *did* know better. He chose, however, to willfully and knowingly disobey God, and he quickly incurred the anger and judgment of the Lord (1 Kings 11:9ff).

The tragedy of Solomon provides an important lesson for all of us. Unless knowledge and wisdom are subjected in obedience to God, they become worthless—and even worse than that. We have often heard the phrase, "A little knowledge is a dangerous thing." Perhaps that is true—but greatly more dangerous is *much* knowledge when it is not controlled by obedience to God.

Now, let's take a brief look at another portion of Scripture, sometimes attributed to Solomon but more likely it is the reflections of a later "wise" man. Note these two pungent observations from one who had drunk deeply from the wells of knowledge and wisdom. "For in much wisdom is much vexation, and those who increase knowledge increase sorrow" (Ecclesiastes 1:18). Then these words that my former students sometimes called to my attention with delight: "Of making many books there is no end, and much study is a weariness of the flesh" (Ecclesiastes 12:12b).

I believe that we have cited enough biblical evidence to indicate that there are definite limits to the worth of knowledge and wisdom, and even some potential dangers. However, these do not deny or nullify the truth that education can also be very beneficial, as outlined earlier in this chapter. Let's turn to Scripture again with this in mind.

Wise men were a recognized professional class in ancient Israel (and throughout the ancient Near East), and Jeremiah 18:18 lists them along with priests and prophets. Those skilled in wisdom were often included among the counselors of kings, and they were able to render a very useful service in this capacity. Unfortunately, some of them were also a bit too inclined to tell the ruler only what he wanted to hear! I am afraid that this still happens today.

Some of the Hebrew wise men, in their role as scribes, also provided an invaluable service by laboriously preparing hand-written copies of Scripture down through the centuries. We are all in their debt. One legitimate and helpful way to honor them is to become good students of the Bible. I should also acknowledge that wise *women* are referred to in the Old Testament. They seemed to have had an important ministry of counseling.

While there are many places in the Old Testament, especially portions of the book of Psalms and the book of Proverbs, that extol the worth of wisdom and knowledge, I would now like to direct our attention to the New Testament. By this time, the Jewish people had established numerous synagogues, with one of their purposes being the provision of an elementary school education for boys. Girls continued to be taught by their parents at home.

We have no information about any type of formal education for Jesus, but he was certainly a very bright boy. When he was twelve years old, he accompanied his parents to Jerusalem for the observance of the festival of Passover. He lingered behind after the celebration was over. When his parents sought him, they found him sitting among learned men in the temple and astounding them with the depth and breadth of his knowledge. When Jesus finally left Jerusalem to return to his home in Nazareth, we are told that he "kept increasing in wisdom and stature, and in favor with God and man" (Luke 2:52, New American Standard Bible).

Jesus, who was not omniscient while in human form,

learned the trade of carpentry, but he must have also been an avid student of the Scripture. Just before he began his public ministry, he withdrew to the Wilderness of Judea where Satan set three temptations before him (see Matthew 4:1-11). Jesus rejected each of these on the basis of Scripture, citing three verses from the book of Deuteronomy. Throughout his ministry, Jesus amazed people with his knowledge (see Matthew 7:28-29 and 13:53-56). And never once did he waver in his total obedience to his Heavenly Father.

In terms of formal schooling, the most learned man in the New Testament is undoubtedly the Apostle Paul. As a Pharisee, he was highly educated in the Scripture and in the teachings of the rabbis. After his conversion to Christianity, Paul became the premier theologian among the earlier follower of Jesus. The book of Romans is one good example of his intellectual brilliance.

Paul believed it was important for Christians to be informed: "And this is my prayer, that your love may overflow more and more with knowledge and full insight, to help you determine what is best, so that in the day of Christ you may be pure and blameless" (Philippians 1:9-10). Notice here his mention of "love." Paul was absolutely sure that without love, knowledge was worthless (see his words in 1 Corinthians 13).

It was certainly helpful to have someone of Paul's ability as a leader in the early church. Paul could more than "hold his own" in discussions with the philosophers, teachers, and the false prophets of his day. And through his numerous writings, which make up a significant part of the New Testament, he was able to set forth clearly the message of God. Another learned man, a physician named Luke, became one of Paul's chief helpers, and he wrote two books that also became a portion of Scripture—The Gospel According to Luke and the book of Acts. The intellectual prowess of these two men bore much worthy fruit because they were unwavering in their commitment and obedience to God.

But what about those who are not highly educated—can they play a worthy role in the advancement of the Kingdom of God? Yes, of course they can! Consider that when Jesus chose his first twelve disciples, many of those selected were fisherman. Remember these words written by Paul to members of the early church in Corinth: "Consider your own call, brothers and sisters: not many of you were wise by human standards, not many were powerful, not many were of noble birth" (1 Corinthians 1:26).

From the beginning, God has invited all persons to participate with him in his work—and historically the majority of these have had only a modest education at best. Those without formal schooling have never been considered unworthy on that basis, nor denied acceptance because of their lack of educational credentials. The Kingdom of God, it seems, has other and more important standards.

Examination Time

Throughout this chapter, we have been raising questions and examining evidence. We have done our homework. Now it is time for us to turn in our reports and take the final examination. What have we learned about education, knowledge, and wisdom? And—how do these relate to the question of worth?

I believe a fair reading of the evidence clearly shows that education can be very helpful and beneficial, and that knowledge and wisdom are worth obtaining. But they should be pursued with honesty and integrity, with worthy motivation, and with care to avoid the pitfalls and dangers along the way. We have seen that knowledge and wisdom can result in serious and tragic consequences unless it is coupled with obedience to God.

There is absolutely no evidence available that shows a direct correlation between the presence of knowledge and wisdom—or the lack of it—and the personal worth of a human being. Education can be exceedingly valuable, but it cannot guarantee to turn us into persons of worth. Knowledge has the power to enhance or erode worth, but not produce it.

Since it seems conclusive that neither money nor knowledge has the power to produce worth, we will have to continue our quest by turning elsewhere. Perhaps what we need to do is find a way to become famous. Now, that's an idea worth looking into!

CHAPTER THREE

Fame and Acclaim

Nearly everyone likes applause; some find it downright intoxicating. Perhaps you have fond memories of a crowd applauding your performance in a school or church play . . . or clapping enthusiastically as you concluded a piano recital . . . or roaring with approval as you helped your ball team win an important game. What was your greatest moment of fame? Did you save any programs or paper clippings? Or is it possible that you, like perhaps the majority of persons, have *no* memories of such times? In that case, hopefully you have received affirmation in other ways. And possibly some of you are enjoying much acclaim right now. If so, how does it make you feel?

Referring again to the game Careers, fame was considered to be one of the three routes to "Success," and, I suppose, to "Worth." Although some points for fame could be earned in numerous ways, three careers were most promising for this purpose: Hollywood, Politics, and Space Travel. Today, one would surely consider adding Professional Athletics—what else would you include? A few folks, of course, are born into "famous" families and they wear that mantle throughout life with ease or discomfort.

Fame and acclaim make us feel like SOMEBODY, and that can often be a good thing. Our question, however, remains: what role do they play in helping us to become persons of true worth? Does anyone have an applause meter calibrated with that in mind? Now, as we remember whatever image the phrase "hill of beans" conjures up in our mind, let us continue our quest to understand the source and nature of real worth. Thus far our success has been rather limited, although I believe that we have learned a lot.

The Quest for Fame

From the beginning of human life on earth, most individuals have been born, lived, and died in obscurity. No trace of their existence has been left behind. Their names are recorded nowhere; there are no sculptures, paintings, or photographs to preserve their likeness. No recordings contain their voices. Perhaps we should pause for a few minutes and reflect on this. (Remember, however, that God knows fully every person who has ever lived.)

Even in recent centuries and in advanced cultures, most persons remain largely unknown. When they die, only a small circle of family, friends, and acquaintances remember them. And in a generation or two, the memory grows dim—and then is gone. Perhaps their names can be found in an old newspaper obituary, or a faded photograph may exist in a school yearbook from long ago—but chances are high that no one will look. (This has changed a little in recent times as more persons have become interested in doing genealogical studies.)

In every period of time, however, a few individuals *do* find wide-spread recognition and positive acclaim. Some of these persons continue to be remembered by succeeding generations. These folks are rightly called "famous." Are they also therefore the persons with greatest worth? Should you and I seek fame? If so, how do we proceed? What have others done?

Persons seek fame for many reasons and look for it in a myriad of places. For some, acclaim itself is a primary motivating factor; for others, it is mainly a by-product. In most cases, I suspect it is a mixture of the two. There are those who avidly seek fame from early life; for others it is not until later that acclaim even becomes an issue. Let's look together at several types of careers that sometimes bring fame.

First, what can we learn from artists and authors? It is unlikely that many of these persons set out to become "famous." They paint and write in response to an inward urge to express themselves in creative ways, and they possess the gifts that allow them to achieve their goals. Some, but certainly not all, are rewarded with acclaim for their work, and at least a few may also become wealthy—they will find "fame and fortune." Interestingly enough, however, it is not uncommon for people pursuing these careers to achieve significant recognition and acclaim only *after* their death. For example, none of the marvelous poems of Emily Dickinson were published during her lifetime.

All in all, it is precarious for artists and authors to embark on their careers with the purpose of becoming rich or famous, but that is rarely their primary motivation. By the way, I have observed that persons who have become famous for other reasons often feel compelled to write a book. In my reading experience, I have reached the conclusion that the majority of such books are very poor in many ways—they would never sell well were it not for the "name" of the author.

Then, there are public performers who in various roles—stage, movies, television, and professional sports—may find themselves on a fast track to acclaim. The allure and prospect of fame is a strong motivating factor for many of these folks. Although they have talents that they feel an inward compulsion to develop and use, the presence of an audience is necessary for success. Performers draw their energy from the approval and applause of others—and this acclaim motivates them to seek higher and higher levels of achievement and recognition.

Hazards abound, however, during the active career of most persons who draw their sustenance from the praise lavished on them by others. I can think of several such dangers, and you will be able to add to the list. One thing that immediately comes to my mind is that some of these persons achieve fame so quickly, and often at such an early age, that they cannot handle it very well. They simply do not have the maturity and the accumulation of enough life experience to be able to assimilate the adulation of the crowd in a way that is not disruptive to their life. We hear of the unfortunate results on a regular basis in the media.

One of the unfortunate and scary things about these failures is that performers are role models for others, especially young people. This is true whether or not "stars" will admit or accept this reality. Their behavior *will be* emulated by many of their fans. It is bad enough for a famous person to go astray—but it is even worse when others follow them in the same destructive paths. The power possessed by a successful performer to influence others for good or bad is immense.

There are other hazards. Those who achieve recognition and acclaim from the crowd not uncommonly discover that they have also provoked much jealousy among others aspiring to fame. Or, lacking success, they become consumed with envy and hard feelings toward those who have received greater recognition than they. Either way, the work place is not always a friendly and happy place. Often it is furnished with insincerity, pettiness, shallowness, and resentfulness. Performers are competitors. Competition may draw out the best in persons—but it can also lead to thoughts and deeds that are less than wholesome and noble.

And then there is this about performers. Their approval base is often rather small. "Stars" secure a niche among their devoted, enthusiastic, vocal, and loyal followers—but there are always many others who remain unimpressed and even disdainful. As I think about famous performers today, a lot of them would be totally unknown if I were the one doing the evaluation! If the way to true worth as an individual is via a route marked "fame and acclaim," it would seem to be a narrow and uncertain path. What if the majority of people ignore our "act"? And even if the majority approve, is worth established on the basis of a popularity contest? The question is worth pondering.

A third area in which public acclaim is frequently found is politics. Politicians tend to share many of the characteristics, both positive and negative, of the public performers just considered. One would like to believe that men and women who aspire to careers in politics do so mainly out of a motivation to render service to the public. There are such individuals (I believe I have known a few), but I fear that this is by no means always the case.

By its very nature, politics attracts those persons who have a big ego and who literally crave the approval of the masses. They are elected to office by majority vote—and the temptation is always strong for them to tell the people "what they want to hear." (On the other hand, politicians often choose as their own close advisors those who will tell them what *they* want to hear.) It is rare for politicians to give straight, direct answers to questions (check this out on television). They have indeed revived the ancient craft of "spinning," although with a new meaning for the term. Their ability to admit mistakes is almost non-existent.

In fairness, politicians have a high level of vulnerability. Many things beyond their control can have an adverse effect on their standing in the public's eye—unfavorable economic patterns, local and national dangers and disasters, unreasonable and changing expectations of them by their constituents, and harsh attacks from their political opponents. The media can be fierce, and candidates always face an uncertain future at each election. All in all, politics is a difficult arena in which to achieve and maintain fame . . . but there is rarely any shortage of individuals attempting to do so! Do you think that ego is largely the reason for this?

More than most persons, politicians (especially at the higher levels) tend to be concerned about their place in history. Such history may ultimately prove to be laudatory or negative. Human historians are fallible, however, and they are certainly not well equipped to evaluate the intrinsic worth of a human being. There is only ONE who can do that.

Now let's consider for a moment a fourth type of career in which fame is occasionally achieved. I am referring to men and women who choose to work in the field of religion. Those who select a career in some type of religious ministry are rarely seeking fame—and if some of them are coveting acclaim, they are sadly out of step with Jesus! The vast majority of religious workers function in the role of a servant, and they try to minister to the hurts and needs of others. They may achieve much more fame than we are aware of—but it is not of an earthly variety.

A few, however, do become famous in the sense that their names are known throughout the world, and their contributions are recognized and respected by future generations of appreciative people. Every age has produced a few such persons. What names come to your mind? I can think of quite a few. Among those in the Christian tradition, I would include Saint Augustine, Thomas Aquinas, Martin Luther, John Bunyan, Billy Sunday, Charles Spurgeon, "General" William Booth, Mother Teresa, Martin Luther King, Thomas Merton, and Billy Graham.

This is a very incomplete list, but it gives some idea of the diversity of types of ministry that can sometimes lead to fame. However, *no one* should *ever* choose a religious vocation with the hope of finding fame and adulation. I can think of almost nothing more unworthy.

There are many other fields of endeavor where at least a few individuals may become highly respected and even find fame. For example, these include business, technology, and the military. However, I will focus briefly on only one more area—the field of science, including medicine.

I believe it unlikely that many of these persons are primarily motivated by a dream to become famous, but once in a while acclaim does come to some of them. Examples would include the physicists Albert Einstein and Madam Curie, the chemist Louis Pasteur, and the physician Jonas Salk. I imagine that you find these names familiar—but how many Nobel Prize winners (in science or other areas) from the last ten years can you name? Only an elite few men and women of science gain general and long-lasting appreciation and recognition.

At first glance, we might be inclined to think that fame, regardless of where it is found, is a highly individual matter. While that is sometimes true, more often than not other persons are involved in the birth of the "star." If we look beyond the person in the spotlight, wherever the stage might be, the size of the supporting cast may surprise us. Many people who rarely receive any personal acclaim or recognition often contribute significantly to the success of the famous person. This group often includes family members, teachers, coaches, and the like.

Here is an example from the Bible. My favorite Old Testament personality is Moses. He was a giant among men, and his fame has been proclaimed for more than three thousand years—not only by members of the Judeo-Christian faith, but by a multitude of other persons. His story occupies much of the biblical books of Exodus, Leviticus, Numbers, and Deuteronomy, but his fame is not confined to the Bible.

Here are two more interesting things about Moses: first, he did not become famous until late in life; second, although arguably the most famous person who has ever lived (excepting, of course, the Incarnate Christ), Moses is said to have been the most humble man on the face of the earth (Numbers 12:3).

Moses, however, was not a self-made man of distinction. Among those who helped him to achieve his remarkable success were his mother, his sister, and his brother. His wife and his father-in-law also were exceedingly helpful to Moses, as were a number of personal friends and associates. God employed *many* persons to help mold this man who towers above most other famous persons. We owe each of them profound gratitude for their contributions.

Contributions of the Famous

Although the benefits, both tangible and unseen, that famous persons enjoy are highly personal, the positive contributions they make to the general public are not negligible. Even if a celebrity happens to be highly self-centered, temperamental, and conceited (as some certainly are), he or she often has much to offer for the enrichment of society. We can accept their gifts gratefully and with integrity, even if we are not particularly fond of the giver.

Throughout this whole section dealing with the contributions of the famous, especially that concerned with entertainers, I recognize that the comments made and examples given are to some extent parochial. They reflect my western hemisphere orientation and my personal tastes. Readers are encouraged to think about the same issues based on their backgrounds and preferences. I have chosen not to include the contributions made by politicians at this point, but I will return to a discussion of political figures in chapter four.

Where shall we begin? Let's think of the famous inventors who have blessed all of us. To mention just a few of those whose names are familiar to most: Alexander Graham Bell (although there are numerous times when I question *this* blessing!), Thomas Edison, Henry Ford, and Orville and Wilbur Wright. In a slightly different category, I was greatly inspired in my youth by the story of George Washington Carver, the "peanut" man, and I still remember him with much appreciation today. These celebrities—and many, many others—have helped shape the world in which we live. Reflect for a few minutes on those most meaningful to you.

In what might be called the realm of culture, society

certainly owes a lot to those talented persons who have made our world a more pleasant place, filling it with beauty and inspiration. To name just a few examples, there are master musicians like Bach, Beethoven, Brahms, Handel, Mozart, and Tchaikovsky. How drab life would be without the work of artists such as DaVinci, Michaelangelo, and Rembrandt. And in the area of great literature, a host of persons immediately leap into my mind because of the blessings I have received from their writings. To cite just a tiny minority, I offer the following ten names: Browning, Bunyan, Dickens, Dickinson, Emerson, Frost, Keats, Shakespeare, Tennyson, and Wordsworth.

Famous entertainers come in many guises and practice a variety of art forms. From early life, I have had a deep affection for radio, and still listen daily—primarily to popular and classical music. When I was a child, I (and many Americans) delighted in following the antics of Fibber McGee and Molly (how could they get so much stuff in that closet!?) and the wit of Jack Benny (what a violin player!). These and other humorists made life a little brighter at a time when there was much darkness.

As far as movies are concerned, my personal support would produce no celebrities since I average seeing only one movie a year—and have been known to walk out on some of these before their conclusion! Although I personally have little interest in this art form, many of my friends enjoy movies very much, and no one can doubt the contributions the motion picture industry has made to our world. People go to movies primarily to be entertained, I suppose, but also to learn, to be inspired, and perhaps at times to temporarily escape the pressures of life. When people are asked to think of a "famous" person, I imagine that many would remember a favorite actor or actress, and the impact that person has had on their life.

Do you enjoy television? The majority of persons do, and once more I find myself in the minority. I rarely watch anything other than news programs. (The last program I watched on a regular basis for entertainment was *Gunsmoke*!) But television has had an enormous influence on countless persons, for better or worse, and the contributions that acclaimed TV personalities have made to modern life cannot be over-estimated.

Since I do not care much for movies and television programs, you might wonder what I do for relaxation, entertainment, and diversion. One significant part of the answer is that I have had an on-going love affair with books since I was six years old. In addition to the inspirational and informative "great" literature that I came to appreciate, mentioned earlier, I enjoy reading many different literary types. High on my list are the murder mysteries written by Agatha Christie, and the imaginative, fantasy literature by C. S. Lewis. Authors, writing in many different forms and styles, have made a huge contribution to my life—and I hope to yours. A few of the other things that I particularly enjoy include conversations with friends, amateur astronomy, riding my bicycle, and hiking—especially in beautiful Yosemite National Park.

Let's move on to sports. Spectators spend an enormous amount of time and money each year avidly following and cheering on their favorite athletes. (Unfortunately, there is a trend now for some athletes and fans to engage in *unworthy* behavior during and after games.) Some of the highest profile and most widely acclaimed persons today are found in professional sports. The contributions made by individuals and teams to the recreation and entertainment of the general population is immense.

Numerous young people have been challenged and inspired to seek careers in some type of athletic endeavor. Athletics—and the entertainment industry as a whole—also contributes to the economy of our nation, especially in the area of clothing sales, as well as through the advertisement of all kinds of products.

Most of the persons in the various categories we have been discussing in this chapter enjoy acclaim when it comes their way. For some, it is their lifeblood. Without this tonic, they have a tendency to wither and fade. But one's time in the limelight does not last forever. What happens when the lights dim and the crowds grow silent . . . when the curtain falls on the final performance?

When the Curtain Falls

An interesting thing about careers leading to fame is that the curtain often falls rather soon. The time of "glory" for athletes, movie and television stars, politicians, and other celebrities is often fleeting indeed. Unless these individuals have also cultivated other interests (and made appropriate financial plans), the period after the acclaim has waned can be long and bleak.

Many people, regardless of whatever career they have followed, find retirement to be deeply satisfying and enjoyable (assuming reasonable health and freedom from too many financial worries). Retirees love the independence now theirs and the opportunity to pursue their own interests. Although they tend to be as busy as ever, they now can often formulate their own agenda and schedule. But retirement years are not happy ones for all persons, and the discontentment and unease that some experience can frequently be traced back to their years in the work force.

All too often, persons unwisely tend to derive their very identity from their work, and this sets the stage for many problems. I think this may be especially true for those who have sought and found fame. These folks are in danger not only of being shaped unduly by their jobs, but also by the perception that others have of them. Their identity to a great extent is commonly derived from their fans—and fans and crowds are notoriously fickle. When one is no longer adored and applauded, life can become difficult and confusing. And one can easily become depressed, and burdened with feelings of failure and *worthlessness*.

I believe most of us can understand, at least partially, how difficult it can be for some famous persons to move to the sidelines, by choice or against their will, and blend into the anonymity of the masses. After a period of being widely recognized and quoted, of being swamped with desirable invitations, of being sought after for autographs and endorsements, and of being at the center of events, life on the periphery could well call for a lot of painful and difficult adjustments. As they see the world moving on, the question might easily arise: "*How can it do that without ME?*" And close behind, other questions: "Who *am* I, anyway—and what am I *worth?*"

For these and other reasons (some may be more valid than others), there have always been men and women celebrities who attempt to regain their former status. They once more seek the spotlight. This is a difficult quest and one that often fails. Even if these persons do achieve "success" once more, one wonders if the consideration of more important issues—such as the determination of what constitutes ultimate value and worth in life—is not being avoided by some. Regardless of who we are, each of us would be wise to seek answers for those questions. None of our friends, constituents, or fans can do it for us. There is Help available, but it does not come from ratings and polls. Perhaps of the possible paths to worth that we have considered thus far (including wealth and education), the search for success through fame is the most precarious. Let's step back and seek some wisdom and guidance in this matter from the only One whose judgment we can trust fully.

A True Perspective

I believe a good way to gain some helpful perspective is to look at some verses in the fortieth chapter of the book of Isaiah (you would find it constructive to read the entire chapter). The prophet is deeply impressed with the majesty of God, and keenly aware of the tremendous difference between God and all human life.

Notice verses 15-17—all of the nations of the earth are like drops of water or specks of dust when compared to God. Reflect on verse 22—all the people of the earth are like grasshoppers when measured by the greatness of God. Be informed by verses 23-24—all of the princes and rulers of the earth are as nothing in the presence of God, and their tenure in power is brief.

Now, this does not mean that nations, peoples, and rulers are unimportant and worthless—far from it. The prophet only seeks to affirm that the achievements, fame and splendor of all human beings pale into insignificance when considered against the backdrop of God's overwhelming majesty and glory. There is a Divine standard for greatness and worth that we would be short sighted and foolish to ignore.

Let us also consider Jesus, God's Divine Son, who once lived among earth's people in human form. From humble and obscure beginnings, Jesus achieved much recognition and adoration from multitudes of people—but only for a while. When the crowds came to realize that this marvelous teacher, this healer of people with all kinds of diseases, and this performer of many great miracles was not going to use his powers to promote an earthly kingdom and free them from the hated Romans, the applause quickly died. The curtain came down with a thud! And there was a crucifixion on the Hill of Calvary.

But it was, of course, beyond the curtain that reality was revealed most clearly and that true greatness and worth were defined forever. The resurrection of Jesus placed the stamp of validity on all that he had taught and done, and pointed the way to a future full of promise and hope. And so it is now. Worth is rarely secured fully by performances occurring while the curtain is up, though these may be legitimate, inspiring, and helpful. What usually matters most is the life that continues after the applause has faded and the curtain has fallen. It is then that worth can be more accurately evaluated. It is also then that the artificial and temporary have an opportunity to be transformed into what is real and permanent.

All of us need a strong, healthy self-esteem. But as the Apostle Paul cautions: "Do not think of yourself more highly than you should. Instead, be modest in your thinking, and judge yourself according to the amount of faith that God has given you" (Romans 12:3b, Today's English Version). I believe Paul's counsel is sound.

No matter how intelligent, gifted, and talented we may be, there are almost certainly those who surpass us. The Psalmist understood that truth quite well and was at peace with himself and God. Ponder his words: "O Lord, my heart is not lifted up, my eyes are not raised too high; I do not occupy myself with things too great and too marvelous for me. But I have calmed and quieted my soul" (Psalm 131:1-2a).

There is, however, another side to this matter. As Paul wisely cautioned, we should not think too highly of ourselves. But—neither should we think too lowly of ourselves. There are far too many persons seriously crippled by a devastatingly low self-esteem. They have a view of themselves that is totally unwarranted. Are you one of those unhappy persons? Let me assure you that you are certainly more important than you feel you are. If you are having serious problems with this matter, I urge you to read *all* of this book. Also, you might find it beneficial to seek professional counseling.

Not too highly . . . not too lowly . . . but just right! That should be our goal. We should also shun a false humility. C. S. Lewis has a very helpful discussion of this in chapter fourteen of *The Screwtape Letters*. Let me quote two of his observations. Evil forces have induced thousands of humans "to think that humility means pretty women trying to believe they are ugly and clever men trying to believe they are fools." That, of course, is *not* humility.

Lewis goes on to note that God wants each person "to be so free from any bias in his own favor that he can rejoice in his own talents as frankly and gratefully as in his neighbour's talents . . . He wants each man, in the long run, to be able to recognize all creatures (even himself) as glorious and excellent." I believe that this is a good and true understanding of humility. Most of us will never become "famous," but we can rejoice in God's love for us as we are—and in whatever nature of person he will help us to become.

The Critic's Review

We have seen that a halo of acclaim, sought or not, rests on the head of certain persons in numerous walks of life. It has also been noticed that those who actively pursue fame encounter many hazards along the way, and often sustain disappointments. A mixture of glory and pain is not uncommon. But famous persons, as we have observed, frequently contribute much of worth to society. Yes, they are contributors of that which may have worth . . . but does fame bring inner, authentic worth to the one who is famous? Does it make a celebrity worth more than a hill of beans?

There is nothing, I believe, that indicates any correlation between acclaim and the possession of worth. There are even special attitudes and characteristics that some famous persons are particularly prone to develop which erode and tarnish personal worth. I think, for example, of pride, selfishness, and arrogance. It must be difficult to remain genuinely humble and demonstrate true humility when there is a loud chorus of voices singing your praise and telling you how WONDERFUL you are. This is just another challenge that many celebrities must face—and hopefully respond to in a healthy and worthy fashion.

The truth is that earthly applause and commendation can never be used to reliably measure the real worth of an individual. In one of my favorite C. S. Lewis books, *The Great Divorce*, the reader is introduced to a woman named Sarah Smith. During her earthly life, Sarah never attracted the attention of the masses, but in heaven she was highly honored and applauded by those who had previously come in contact with her on earth, and who had been blessed by the quality of her life. In heaven, these very significant comments are made about her: "She is one of the great ones. Ye have heard that fame in this country and fame on Earth are two quite different things" (chapter twelve). Yes, indeed!

As I was working on this section of *A Hill of Beans*, I received a special issue of a popular newsmagazine (*Time*, April 26, 2004). This issue is devoted to a presentation of the 100 most powerful and influential persons in the world today, the famous and a few of the "infamous." Obviously, such a selection was very difficult to make—and probably no reader is fully happy with the result.

As I read through the pages with interest, I thought again about the fortieth chapter of Isaiah (mentioned earlier)—and also of Sarah Smith. Without wanting to belittle the persons on *Time's* list, I wondered this—Who are the 100 most powerful and influential persons in the world today as seen through the lens of eternity and from the vantage point of heaven? I believe the whole meaning of "powerful" and "influential" would need to be re-defined in order to begin to respond to this question. And surely one would need to consider how these words relate to "worth."

Thus far we have considered the accumulation of wealth, the acquisition of knowledge, and achievement of fame as possible ways to find personal worth. None of these has proved to be very satisfactory. All three, however, share something important. Each, in its own way, bestows *power* on the possessor. Could it be that this is the key we have been looking for? Perhaps we need to consider more closely the question of the relationship between power and worth.

CHAPTER FOUR

Power

A "hill of beans" has minimal value and certainly no discernible power. It has become a metaphor for that which isn't worth much. But if in some way (maybe a miraculous new plant food!) it could be infused with power, would it then have worth? If so, could the same thing happen to us?

Let's proceed with a series of other questions. Take time to reflect on each one. I will join you. How much power does each of us actually have? How did we acquire this power? Do we wish we had more? How do we really feel about power—our own and that of others? On balance, have our experiences with power been more positive than negative? What undesirable encounters have we had with power?

Power exists in many guises, but there are two forms that are most common—power as *ability* and power as *authority*. The first type of power is that which gives one the ability and capacity to accomplish desired objectives. The second type of power gives one authority. This may include control over other persons. These two kinds of power often merge and intermingle.

But where is power to be found? Why do some people have it and others don't? Assuming that you and I believe power might possibly be beneficial for us to have, how available (and expensive) is it, and where do we go to find this commodity? Let's explore the more usual sources.

Avenues to Power

Back in chapter two, we investigated the importance of education, especially as it related to personal worth. Now let's think about it with reference to power. Education, formal and sometimes informal, provides the foundation in most cases for power of all types. The unlearned and the ignorant are usually excluded from the ranks of the powerful. Society should encourage and enable its citizens to obtain an appropriate education—everyone will benefit.

In ancient Sumer, as we have seen, boys of the upper classes went to school in order to obtain the preparation necessary for them to qualify for responsible positions in government offices and temples. Without this training, they could not fulfill their potential and the hopes of their families. They studied diligently to obtain the ability (power) needed to achieve their ambitions, and countless others have followed in similar paths.

I have some personal understanding of this process. As an economically poor youngster growing up in the Missouri Ozarks, I had the "wild" idea that I could become a physician. Obviously the power to achieve this hope would be available only through education. The road to the coveted M.D. degree was long and arduous, but eventually I held the diploma, a symbol of a fulfilled dream, in my hands. Now I had the ability and authority to practice my chosen profession. Many of you, I am sure, have found that it was education, academic or vocational, that empowered you to achieve your goals.

True education is much more than the accumulation of facts and the development of specific skills. It contributes to the acquisition of desirable social graces, and also to the enhancement of personal qualities such as poise, confidence, and self-esteem—attributes that enhance the achievement and employment of power. One aspect of this that has tremendous importance for obtaining and exercising power involves fluent speech.

In the ancient world, one of the most highly regarded assets a person could have was the ability to speak well. In ancient Egypt, for example, facility with the spoken word could lift an individual out of the quagmire of humble origins and poverty, and set that person on the avenue to respect, achievement, and authority. Much the same remains true today. A speech course, preferably in high school, will pay big dividends.

The Bible, especially the book of Proverbs, has much to say about the value and importance of speech. For example, "A word fitly spoken is like apples of gold in a setting of silver" (Proverbs 25:11). However, it is also important to know when *not* to speak. Ancient wisdom instructs us that there is "a time to keep silence, and a time to speak" (Ecclesiastes 3:7b). And there is this humorous reminder: "Even fools who keep silent are considered wise; when they close their lips, they are deemed intelligent" (Proverbs 17:28)!

For the person who would seek power, a wise place to begin is to build a solid foundation consisting of a good education. While not all individuals considered persons of power by society are well educated, I believe those who do not have a good education are in the minority. But what types of careers built on this foundation are most likely to lead to power?

Well, in one sense, any honorable career can be considered powerful if one's ambitions and goals are achieved. Remember, one important type of power is that which gives you and me the *ability* to accomplish our objectives. This is the most common variety of power and it can provide us enormous satisfaction, and can also give us a positive feeling that our life has purpose—and perhaps worth. It also allows us to contribute to the welfare and good of other persons.

Perhaps a word of caution is in order. There is one common reason why education and training do not always lead to the fulfillment of a person's established goals. A characteristic of almost all truly powerful persons is that they are industrious—they work very hard at their tasks. Laziness and power do not go together. Sloth and achievement are mutually exclusive. On the other hand, some people become workaholics and that is certainly not a good thing either. (For further reading about work, I recommend the chapter "Off to Work We Go" in my book, *Less Than a Mile*.)

Here is another word of caution: power and authority are too often sought in dubious (to say the least!) ways. It is not uncommon for students to cheat on exams and other projects. Some athletes have been found to use unlawful "performance enhancing" substances. Job seekers have been known to falsify resumes and to conceal information. Employees often try to struggle up the corporate ladder by the use of ruthless and dishonorable tactics. Politicians sometime reach for elected positions by deception and through the manipulation of data.

In these and numerous other situations, the slogan seems to be: "Power At Any Price!" Well, power can certainly be achieved in unworthy ways, and it may include a high level of authority. Yes, that is true. But can it thereby result in an increase in personal worth? I think not. Make no mistake—we cannot produce a noble garment out of the tattered rags of lies, deceit, greed, and lust. It just cannot be done, no matter how hard we try or how tightly we close our eyes to the truth.

Let us entertain the idea, however, that we *would* like to possess power as *authority* and that our motivation and intentions are honorable. What options might be open for us to consider? Powerful persons with authority can, of course, be found in the upper echelons of numerous jobs and professions, including those who have found fame in the entertainment industry, but let's consider only three of the more usual places where power, as authority, tends to be concentrated. If we believe that power can lead to worth, we will not want to ignore any of these. Whether or not we choose to invest our life here is quite another matter!

Let's begin with the broad field of journalism, which is defined in my desk dictionary (*Webster's II, New College Dictionary*) as "the collection, writing, editing, and dissemination of news through the media." Almost every word in that definition breathes power! By media, I am referring to various types of printed material, especially newspapers, as well as radio and television. The authoritarian power of the media derives from its capability to shape information, and its opportunity to influence the thinking of the public through its control of the news.

Totalitarian nations grant very little freedom to the media—that would be far too dangerous for their agenda! Instead, they control the media and use it as a potent agent of propaganda. Fortunately, in the United States, the First Amendment to the Constitution protects the freedom of the press, along with freedom of speech and some other basic rights we have as citizens.

Almost every journalist has the possibility of attaining at least a modest degree of power. Some become very powerful—their influence is wide spread, and many people consider their observations and pronouncements authoritative. A few journalists have an unusually potent blend of education, wealth, fame—and power. Their stature is too large to be ignored. Journalism can be a promising career for those who are comfortable with power in varying amounts and who will use it for the good of the public.

We should be grateful for dedicated and talented journalists. There are, however, some things worth remembering. All is not perfect in the domain of journalism. We need to be aware of the fact that the media sometimes distorts information (perhaps in a race to be the first to bring us "breaking news"). The tendency is also very great for the media to use sensationalism in an attempt to gain and keep our attention. Also, we must never forget that all news items in the media have been selected for us, leaving us to wonder what has been left out that might be of importance.

I have a few suggestions for those of us who are the "customers" of the media. Remember that news agencies do pay attention to circulation figures and ratings, so we are not entirely powerless. Here are three recommendations. First, I believe we should *diversify*. By this I mean that we should be careful not to obtain all of our information from the same type of media. For example, we can mix print media and television—but let's be careful not to listen to only one channel or network. Consider including the Public Broadcasting Service (PBS) among your options. Diversification will give us a wider selection of news stories, and also a useful variation in points of view.

Then, let's *discriminate* as we read and listen. Communication is a two-way process, and we should learn to be careful readers and listeners. As we all know, something is not necessarily true or accurate just because we read it in the newspaper, or heard it on the radio (television). Let's be discriminating in our analysis of news reports and in our search for the truth. (And be very skeptical of all those commercials!)

Third, we would be wise to *discuss* the news with other people—and not just those who are almost certain to share our point of view. An honest comparison of our understanding of news reports with that of our friends, neighbors, and fellow workers can be illuminating. Also, let's not be reluctant to share our thoughts, positive and negative, with appropriate representatives of the media. I have personally found greater success in communicating with journalists than I have with politicians!

I suggest that we now move on to the area of politics. This offers many possibilities to consider on the local, state, and national level. Among the more illustrious possessors of authority we would find mayors, governors, legislators, judicial figures, and even presidents—one can have dreams and sometimes they come true! There is no doubt that these persons possess a degree of power and authority that can be immense. Perhaps that is one reason there is rarely a dearth of candidates vying for these positions. The Apostle Paul taught that political authority is to be respected and accepted (Romans 13:1-7), except, of course, when to obey such authority would mean disobedience to God.

Holding a political office does give one an opportunity to work for important and constructive causes. There is always a need for honest, capable and dedicated men and women in the field of politics. If you and I should be drawn in this direction, and if we are willing to take the risks involved, we may find power that makes it possible for us to accomplish some truly worthwhile tasks.

Let's not forget, however, that politicians are public figures and are always under scrutiny. Sooner or later, any flaws and undesirable traits they might possess will probably be exposed. The glare of publicity can be particularly detrimental to children in the family. Politics is an important avenue to power—but think it over carefully before you choose to follow that route, and remember the concerns I expressed about politicians in chapter three. Perhaps there is yet another way to power? Could it be money?

"When my ship comes in . . ." "When my rich uncle dies . . ." "When I win the lottery . . ." How do *your* financial fantasies begin? Such speculation can be fun and is usually harmless. A fantasy can be fun to visit, but one must not try to live there. We know that mythological ships never dock. Our rich uncle probably doesn't exist (or will lose his money in the stock market!). The chance that we will win the lottery is infinitesimal. Most of us know this is true. We also know that the only probable way to wealth is through work. But what kind of work? Obviously not just any old job will do.

A third place we might explore in our search for power as authority is the field of big business, where there are promising jobs and where one commonly encounters wealthy persons. And there can be no doubt that very rich individuals and families possess a wand that they can wield with great authority—and in a fashion that often brings other persons under their control. The poor generally have little power, as usually defined, whereas the wealthy ordinarily possess a great deal of power. A career in big business might indeed bring us wealth, power, and authority.

I imagine that most of us, however, are content to possess very little power of the type that gives a high level of authority. The pomp and circumstance often associated with that kind of power has little personal appeal for us. We don't *need* it—and we may be glad to escape associated responsibilities and hazards. We are not sure that the prize is worth the cost, and we may doubt that any avenue to power will actually lead to an increase in our true worth.

The personal possession of power actually makes some individuals quite uncomfortable. When a new job, or a promotion, places them in a position of authority over others, they can become confused and uncertain of themselves. Some folks are just more at ease when they are following others and working under their direction. They don't want a leadership role, and they dislike giving orders.

These persons can become acutely disturbed if they have to take disciplinary action against someone in their charge, or if they have to terminate a worker's employment. Those who struggle with issues of this nature owe it to themselves—and to the ones for whom they are responsible—to find a suitable resolution to their problem. In some cases, this could involve professional counseling, or even a change of job.

On the other hand, there are lots of persons who *do* want power and authority. Some of these individuals become frustrated when they realize that they cannot compete effectively in a large arena. They will never hold a highly visible and esteemed position or a powerful public office. They will never amass a huge fortune. But many of these ambitious persons cannot shed their lust for power.

Therefore, they seek ways to become "a big frog in a small pond." After all, if a tiny enough "pond" can be found (a little town, a small business, a church, one's family), almost anyone has the opportunity to become a person with at least some authority. But whatever the scale may be, power should always be exercised in a responsible and worthy manner. Unfortunately, this does not always happen.

The Use of Power

"Nothing touches us more profoundly for good or for ill than power" (Richard J. Foster, *The Challenge of the Disciplined Life: Christian Reflections on Money, Sex, & Power*, chapter ten). Foster's words set the issue squarely before us. Power is a two-edged sword that can be employed in tremendously helpful ways, but it can also be used to cause terrible destruction. Perhaps it should bear a banner reading: "Caution! Handle With Care!" This warning is especially cogent when authority over others is being exercised.

Envision with me a few of those persons who can and do use their ability and authority to bless others. I think, for example, of teachers who help open minds to the world and its promise (and dangers) . . . composers and performers who provide inspiration and beauty through the power of music . . . philanthropists who give generously to worthy causes . . . medical personnel who alleviate suffering and restore health . . . politicians who labor to enhance safety and quality of life for citizens . . . and pastors who are sources of guidance and comfort. And surely we are grateful for skillful auto mechanics, plumbers, and electricians.

Most of us could easily compile a long list of those who have used their power to help us along our way. If I were to make such a list, there is no doubt whose names would be in first place. I am fortunate indeed that I can honestly place three persons at the top: my parents, who always exercised their ability and authority with wisdom and love, and my wife, Marian, who did me "good, and not harm, all the days of her life" (Proverbs 31:12), and whom I shall love forever and ever.

Others have helped us and we should be thankful—and I believe all of us who possess power of any variety should seek and *find* ways to render aid to others and to assist and empower those in need. While much of this can probably be accomplished through wisely employing our abilities and skills (and authority) as part of our regular work, I feel strongly that we need to do more than this. Everyone should spend some time and energy for the well being of others without expecting or accepting any monetary reward. There will be, however, the reward of a great joy that comes from knowing that we have made a positive contribution to the life of someone else. Often we are blessed more than the one we are blessing. Everyone wins!

Many professional persons, lawyers and doctors for example, have traditionally done a certain amount of *pro bono* work. As mentioned in chapter one, this practice is to be commended. I know a number of persons, following several different careers, who volunteer some of their time and skill to help others learn the English language, and others yet who provide transportation for needy persons to receive medical care or to shop. I also have friends who volunteer to teach helpful classes to inmates at San Quentin prison.

Almost everyone has some skill and gift that he or she

can share to help others—and to empower those persons with a richer and fuller life. Again I affirm what I believe to be a basic and important truth—*each* of us will be very wise to perform some service and devote some portion of our power for the benefit of others without any expectation of being repaid in dollars and cents. By the way, without going into details, I have for many years followed this advice in several different ways. In this matter, at least, I really do practice what I preach! And I have never been sorry.

Our power as individuals can also be used on a broader scope. For example, there is the work place, where many of us spend much of our time, and where struggles for power, and abuses of power, are all too common. Here is an opportunity for us to let our voice be heard, although it might entail some risk. Many good causes involve risk! Discrimination and harassment of any type is completely *unacceptable*—and a *good* use of our power is to make it abundantly clear that such practices will not be tolerated.

Then there is the sphere of civic life. There is usually a strong temptation to feel that one ordinary person has little or no chance of making a difference in political processes and structures. That attitude needs to be resisted. We often have more power than we realize. In any event, we need to be informed about the issues and should let our views be known in appropriate ways, including personal conversations, phone calls, e-mails, and letters. (You can learn a lot about politicians by the way they answer your correspondence!) The power of the ballot is huge. We must always vote. Our one vote *can* make a difference.

Closer to home—quite literally—is our family. The often-heard statement that the family is the basic building block of society is not trite—it expresses a profound truth.

The home is the most important of all places for the good components of power to be exercised. A failure here is very serious indeed, and each person present has a role to play in making the home the best of all places.

Family members have an opportunity to recognize gifts in one another and to encourage their development. Among other things, this engenders self-esteem and confidence, as well as an appreciation for others. Parents have the responsibility of trying to discern any unworthy or unhealthy thoughts children might harbor, and of using their power wisely to challenge and redirect as needed. Above all, the home is where love ought to flourish—and it is also the place where one should have the opportunity to observe and learn how to practice power in constructive ways.

Sadly, however, it is in the home that serious misuse of power often occurs. The abuse of children by parents is all too common. Spouses may seek tyrannical control over one another. Siblings sometimes jockey for favored positions in ways that seek to discredit brothers and sisters. "Big frogs" can cause immense damage in a "small pond," and everyone is hurt—including the "big frog."

Let me illustrate that last comment. In *Appointment With Death*, Agatha Christie tells the story of Mrs. Boynton, a widow who ruthlessly controlled not only the purse strings, but also every moment and each tiny detail of the lives of her four children and her daughter-in-law. A person outside the family, a young physician named Sarah, correctly analyzed this "big frog." "Suddenly, she saw the old woman as a pathetic, ineffectual figure. To be born with such a lust for power, such a desire for dominion—and to achieve only a petty domestic tyranny!" These are words from chapter eight of a book of fiction—but they are all too frequently played out, with variations, in many homes in the real world. (Incidentally, when Mrs. Boynton was "polished off," no one was sorry! I will not tell you "who dun it"!)

Power can be dangerous; authority is a strong intoxicant. The person drunk with power is a hazard both to self and to others. Many years ago, historian Lord Acton (1834-1902) remarked: "Power tends to corrupt, and absolute power corrupts absolutely." History confirms the truth of this observation, which is probably most obvious in the life of certain world political leaders, past and present. A classic example would be Adolf Hitler (whose skill with the spoken word was one key reason for his "success"). But the same principle is at work in lesser figures—the more power *any* person possesses, the higher the danger level is.

It is not only individuals, however, who are liable to abuse power. Institutions, organizations, and business firms tend to be susceptible to the corrupting influence of power. Society is always vulnerable and safeguards are necessary. For example, many laws have been enacted to curtail various misuses of power by big business, but these have not always been fully effective. Exploitation for profit is a problem that just doesn't go away. But how much of "net" worth is "true" worth? What is power really worth?

Power and Worth

Actually, as we have seen, power, despite its hazards, can be worth a great deal. We must always remember its positive benefits to us as individuals and to the larger society in which we live. Let's seek to be realistic about the limits and dangers of power, but at the same time not let ourselves become overly pessimistic and cynical.

As I reflect on this matter, some of the *most* powerful persons I know lack a higher education and have only modest financial means. Their names rarely, if ever, are found in newspapers. Yet they are obviously persons with power and they exude a quiet authority. What is the source of this strength that radiates from their life?

The first word that comes to my mind is *goodness*. They are *good* persons—not perfect (no one is), but undeniably good. There are many facets to their goodness. To name just a few of these, I include transparency, humility, gentleness, authenticity, and morality. And they have a high level of generosity—not just in the use of any financial assets they might have, but especially a generosity of spirit and attitude toward other people. One trait that is missing, but found much too often in persons with other kinds of power, is arrogance.

They are persons that you know you can trust and that you enjoy being around. They bless you by their very presence—and you soon become aware of a strength that makes the power possessed by many other "greater" persons seem paltry and meager. You realize that this "good" power does not seek to intimidate, belittle, exploit, or threaten.

What is the source of this goodness? Let's check in the New Testament. Jesus once said that no one is good except God (Matthew 19:17). *All* that is good, wherever it is found, has its origin in God. In the case of Christians (where I believe this virtue has the only opportunity to reach its most mature form), goodness is produced by the Holy Spirit at work in their life—see Galatians 5:22-23 (the Greek word for "goodness" in verse 22 can also be translated "generosity," as is done in some versions of

Scripture—goodness and generosity go hand in hand).

Goodness is built on the foundation of *love*. In the list of the fruit of the Spirit found in Galatians 5:22-23, love is mentioned first and is to be understood as the source of the other eight fruits listed, including goodness. Once more, we are driven back to God, for the Bible says that God *is* love (1 John 4:16); it is the essence of whom he is. And we must affirm that all true love has its source in God. Goodness and love come from God, and so, too, does all *true* power—wherever it is found and in all the ways it is manifested.

Through the power of his spoken word, God created the cosmos. I suggest that you read and reflect on the words found in Genesis 1:1-31 (notice that God's use of his power led to that which was *good*) and those in John 1:1-3. All that God created he continues to sustain and exercise authority over. In beautiful and bold poetic imagery, a prophet has declared that God knows the stars by name (which indicates his authority over them) and when he calls them to come out at night, "because he is great in strength, mighty in power, not one is missing" (Isaiah 40:26b). On earth, God is the one who sets limits for the sea, saying "so far and no further! Here your powerful waves must stop" (Job 38:11, Today's English Version).

Sometimes, God uses mighty rulers of the earth to accomplish his purposes, even though they may be unaware of this. A case in point is Cyrus, ruler of the Persian Empire in the sixth century B.C. God employed this powerful king to free the Hebrew people from their exile in Babylon, but Cyrus did not know that it was God who equipped him for this task. You can read the interesting account of this in Isaiah 45:1-7.

God, exercising his wisdom, often chooses "the weak

things of the world to shame the things which are strong" (1 Corinthians 1:27b, New American Standard Bible). I believe it is clear that "weak" and "strong" are defined differently in the Kingdom of God than they are in the kingdoms of this earth. But whether weak or strong, one thing is certain: "At the name of Jesus every knee should bend, in heaven and on earth and under the earth" (Philippians 2:10). One day that will come to pass.

If we choose, God will give us power (authority) to become his children (John 1:12). And whenever we find ourselves tired and weak, we have this promise: "Those who trust in the Lord for help will find their strength renewed" (Isaiah 40:31a). This involves much more than just physical strength. God, the proclaimer of the Ten Commandments and the Sermon on the Mount, is the source of all moral power, and he will give his obedient children the wisdom, desire, and energy to live in honorable and ethical fashion.

In addition, then, to power as ability and power as authority—and perhaps sometimes existing along with these two types—it would seem that there is also a power of *being*. This is the kind of power found in those who are truly "good," and it flows from an inward fountain of love that reaches out to bless and refresh other persons. This power is both immense and incorruptible—for it is born of God. A power of this nature without any doubt has *worth*. The old saying, "Might Makes Right," is malicious and false—but the reverse is *true*.

Reading the Meter

Once a month, a worker from the power utility company reads a meter at my house. Soon thereafter, the amount of electricity I have used is concisely reported to me in terms of kilowatt-hours. As I write these words, I am also contemplating buying a new car. One of the statistics provided me by the salesperson is the car's horsepower. I realize, however, that power of the nature we have been discussing in this book does not lend itself to such tidy measurement. This side of heaven, the nature and dimensions of true (and false) power will remain beyond our ability to fully calculate.

Nonetheless, based on our study, I believe some conclusions are justified. We have seen that the forms of power that have been considered are important and can be used to help accomplish many worthwhile tasks. We have also observed that power can be terribly misused and abused. It can be used to help or to harm, and the one who possesses power bears an awesome responsibility.

I have suggested that the greatest power is not that which is achieved by personal effort, as good as that can be, but rather that which flows naturally from the life of a good person. The usual varieties of power may help us live a more effective life, but as I examine the evidence I find *nothing* to indicate that such power can produce personal worth. It seems to be the other way around—persons who *have* worth will also gain a wholesome kind of power.

Our search for the source of worth must continue. Maybe it is just a matter of looking for and finding happiness! Somehow that idea sounds quite attractive. Possibly most of us have said at one time or another, "I don't really need to be rich, smart, famous, or powerful. I just want to be happy." But what do we mean by "happy," and will happiness bring us worth?

CHAPTER FIVE

I Just Want to Be Happy

The words "happy" and "happiness" are not easy to define. Dictionaries commonly suggest that a happy person is one who experiences pleasure and possesses joy. I don't find this particularly illuminating—at least, it doesn't satisfy me. The words "pleasure," and especially "joy," are themselves difficult to understand. Yet, in a general way, and allowing for a huge number of individual variations, I suppose most of us have formed a working concept of what "happiness" means to us personally. When were *you* most happy? *Why* were you happy then?

According to Abraham Lincoln, "Most people are about as happy as they make up their minds to be." This is a good observation and has some validity. I believe, however, that it over-simplifies a very complex issue. There are at least two places where Lincoln's remark deserves closer attention.

First, if you and I wanted to do so, we could tell other people how much money we have in the bank, and also how many years we went to school (and possibly our grades and the results of our IQ tests!). In addition, we could call attention to any indicators, assuming that there are some, which reveal us to be possessors of fame and power. Happiness, however, resists any simple attempts to identify and measure. Quite often, we are not really sure whether we are happy or not!

Second, to "make up our minds," especially when we are not sure what it is that we want, is often a very difficult thing to do. In general terms, some people have a disposition—a product of both genetic endowment and environmental factors—which causes them rather naturally to be cheerful, sunny, positive, optimistic, and apparently happy individuals (but appearances can be deceiving).

Others, with a different make-up and set of experiences, may tend to be dour, gloomy, negative, and pessimistic. Any significant change in their outlook on life will often require more than their simply "making up their minds" to do so. Professional counseling may help—and so can a vital, growing relationship with the Supreme Counselor.

A large assortment of words probably come to mind when we think of happiness—perhaps words such as carefree, freedom, contentment, gladness, satisfaction, health, opportunity, faith, hope, love, and peace. Many of us would surely think also of words like family and friends. Perhaps some of us will admit that we find the words wealth, prestige, and possessions on our list. One thing for sure—if we combined all of the results of our attempts to "define" happiness, we would have a very long document. Quite possibly, we would also discover that happiness for some of us would be thought of primarily as the *absence* of certain factors.

Some persons decide early in life to make happiness, as they understand it, their primary goal. This influences their choice of work, where they choose to live, and their lifestyle. Many of these persons reject the importance of wealth, fame, and power. They often seek to live as simply as possible, and they look for happiness in small things. These are folks who "just want to be happy" and sometimes they appear to have succeeded in their quest—sometimes, but not always.

On the other hand, there are those who make an early decision "to be successful" in life, only to discover later that "success" has brought them less satisfaction than they had hoped for. Whatever they found at the end of their rainbow left them feeling empty, and perhaps even confused, bitter, and depressed. Longings for greater happiness—or a different kind of happiness—bubbled to the surface. At this point, such persons often make career changes, sometimes associated with definite modifications in their lifestyle.

Very few persons, I suppose, want to be *unhappy*. Does happiness, however, merit being made one's major goal, or should it be incorporated into a larger plan? Granted the difficulty of defining happiness, and recognizing that it means different things to different persons, how can happiness be achieved? Will happiness make us persons of worth? Let's go on a journey—maybe we can find the "happy trail," the one that will be just right for each of us.

Paths to Happiness

Perhaps you recall these words from the Declaration of Independence (I have added the italics): "We hold these truths to be self-evident, that all men are created equal, that they are all endowed by their Creator with certain unalienable Rights, that among these are Life, Liberty, *and the pursuit of Happiness*." We affirm in no uncertain terms our God-given right to pursue happiness, but a question arises immediately—how does one find this elusive quality of life?

I have previously mentioned a board game called Careers. I am looking at my old set as I write these words. It is copyright 1955 and the game is, I believe, no longer in production—but I still find it of interest. In this game, one of the three ways to be successful in life is to find happiness (you might remember that the other two ways are the accumulation of wealth and the achievement of fame). It is interesting to see how a player can earn "happiness" points.

A quick way to gain some of these points is to buy a new car—and the more money you spend to purchase the vehicle, the more points you earn! (I believe this idea is still very much alive.) An even quicker way to gain happiness points is to buy a yacht. Once again, the more you pay for the vessel the more happiness you accrue. In fact, the purchase of the most expensive yacht yields *one-fifth* of the total points needed to have a successful career built on happiness—and to win the game.

There is no doubt that numerous people take a materialistic view toward happiness. The more possessions and "toys" they can accumulate, at whatever age, the happier they expect to be. This is part of the appeal of Christmas and birthdays for youngsters, and the desire for "things" usually continues to become stronger as one grows older. The lure for things can be particularly strong in those who experienced poverty in their childhood and who may be out to prove to themselves and others that they are "somebody."

When I was a child, toys were relatively scarce in my home. I improvised and made many of my own, putting them together using simple materials close at hand. They were fun to play with and usually lasted for a long time. Today it is quite different. Stores are full of toys for children of all ages. Most are expensive and can become obsolete very quickly. I am dubious about the degree of happiness these toys generate in their owners. Everyone needs some toys, but their number and expense are open to question.

Items that are genuinely useful and helpful—even necessary in modern society—often move into the "toy" category with amazing speed and ease. I think, for example, of the relationship some persons have with their phones, cameras, and computers, and a host of other high tech items that can probably be best classified as gadgets. In a modern day game of Careers, I wonder how many happiness points would be awarded for the purchase of these items? I imagine it would be quite a few. This seems to be a well-traveled trail by those searching for happiness.

One possession that people have longed for and dreamed about in most ages, and certainly now, is a house. As one might expect, the anticipated degree of satisfaction is usually tied closely to the size, opulence, and expense of the property. Also, we seem to have embraced the very dubious idea that if one house is good, then surely two or three places that we can call home will elevate our happiness to an even higher level.

Celebration of Discipline: The Path to Spiritual Growth is an exceedingly helpful book by Richard J. Foster. In a chapter on "The Discipline of Simplicity," Foster offers this wise counsel: "When you are considering an apartment, a condominium, or a house, thought should be given to livability rather than how much it will impress others." I agree completely. All too many persons, including lots of Christians, have larger (and more ostentatious) houses than they will ever need. In ancient Egypt, the word "pharaoh" meant "big house." Since kings always had the biggest houses, "Pharaoh" soon became used as their title.

Egyptian kings, however, are not remembered for being especially happy persons. How many modern-day "Pharaohs" do you know?

The accumulation of "stuff"—of all kinds and of varying degrees of usefulness—is a well-worn path that countless people have followed in their search for happiness and a feeling of personal worth. There are some, however, for whom this has little attraction. In Agatha Christie's book, *Crooked House*, the reader meets a woman named Clemency, one of those persons who want desperately to be happy, but for whom money has no appeal. Clemency provides an example of those who "dislike luxury, prefer austerity, and are suspicious of possessions." She may be in the minority, but she is certainly not alone. What are other ways to search for happiness?

There are always those persons who seek to find happiness through their work. Many will claim that their greatest joy is provided by the career they have chosen, whatever its nature might be. Some, but certainly not the majority, choose jobs where they are able to exercise a direct ministry to other persons—perhaps as a health care provider or a religious worker. These are persons who elect to put in a lot of overtime, rarely take vacations, and often defer retirement for as long as possible. Although they may have lots of money (possibly with associated power) and many possessions, all of this is secondary in importance to their jobs. Their vocation is what makes their world go around, seemingly—and perhaps actually—in a happy whirl.

On the other hand, a great many persons view their jobs as a sort of "necessary evil," and they often choose their career with this in mind. These folks seek for happiness in their leisure hours, which they guard carefully.

Weekends are cherished, vacations are of supreme importance, and retirement is looked forward to with relish. In Careers, a Florida vacation gains the player four happiness points (I wonder how many a cruise would be worth?). Whatever the destination, many people tend to focus a lot of their time and energy on "getting away" from the routine of their work, for that is what makes them most happy. They tend to spend their money on travel and not on possessions.

Although certainly not restricted to this category of persons, those who pursue leisure often also have a distinct penchant for luxury. They are encouraged by advertisers to pamper and indulge themselves because they are "worth it." Trips to a spa (and maybe a plastic surgeon), purchase of costly cosmetics, and meals at expensive restaurants are very important to some. Leisure and luxury—these two seem to be natural companions for many of those who are searching for happiness (and perhaps eternal youth?).

Then, there have always been those folks who are *unusually* determined to "get away." They look for happiness in secluded areas, want little contact with other persons, and earn their (often) meager income in ways that interfere least with their personal pursuit of that which makes them happy. They tend to be keenly aware of the wonders and beauty of the natural world, and some may be quite creative persons, especially in various types of artistic and literary endeavors. The nature of society today, however, has made it increasingly difficult for anyone to live this type of lifestyle. Those who are able to live this way are often regarded with suspicion by other persons.

Perhaps the majority of people seek happiness in what might be considered a balanced way—in the ebb and flow of "normal" life. They work at jobs that bring a degree of satisfaction, and not a few of the women choose to be full-time homemakers. Leisure time is usually invested in simple activities such as movies, concerts, reading, athletics events, golfing, bicycle rides, hiking, picnics, and the like. Gardening may be a favorite activity. "Family" is considered important, and weddings and the birth of children are occasions for rejoicing. Time with friends is valued. These folks believe that happiness can be found close at hand.

We have briefly examined some of the more common "happiness trails." (I have chosen to leave out those pursuits that are clearly beyond the pale—such as sexual misconduct, abuse of alcohol, and drug addiction, none of which can ever lead to true happiness). What others would you add? I believe it is now time to think about some of the pitfalls along the way of these trails, and to evaluate the degree of success to which these paths are apt to lead us. You might want to consider this in terms of your own experience.

The Downside of Happiness

"I just want to be happy." That sounds entirely reasonable. Those words, however, make me uneasy, and alarms start ringing in my mind. Although I understand the sentiment behind the words, and even though they strike a responsive chord in my own heart, they also arouse a feeling of discomfort within me that just won't go away. There are numerous reasons for this. Some are rather obvious, while others are more subtle, but of crucial importance.

Once again we face this question: What do we mean when we use the word "happy"? *Whatever* it means to us, several additional questions are spawned that each one of us should try to answer. Is what I understand by "happiness" a worthy goal? How much am I willing to sacrifice to be happy, and how might this impact other persons? Is happiness, as I understand it, likely to be attainable? What happens if I fail? These are rather elementary but important questions that we should attempt to answer if we are intent on seeking happiness.

There are many difficulties associated with a search for personal happiness. One of the problems is this—even if we should be fortunate enough to attain what we believed would make us happy, we may well find ourselves disappointed. The advanced academic or professional degree, that coveted job, a full "toy" chest, or an isolated cabin in the woods, to mention just a few examples, may be ours. Yet, we might well have to admit that, for some reason, the happiness we expected to find is sadly lacking. Our search for happiness, although "successful," has actually left some of us feeling quite unhappy. This is a very common story.

Consider also that happiness structured around fame and power is especially vulnerable to loss. It can fade away more quickly than the vapor trail of a jet plane in a windy sky, leaving us feeling empty and forlorn. The pleasure derived from "time off" may be even more transient. The days of a vacation rush by, and part of the happiness of those days is drained away by our realization that the calendar is marching relentlessly toward that time when we will once more have to resume our usual duties. Time seems always to be against us!

Also, we live in light of an ultimate reality. If we seek happiness in terms of what this world has to offer—fame, power, pleasure, possessions, and whatever other treasures appeal to us—we will one day have to leave them all behind. This word of counsel from Jesus is worth remembering: "Do not store up for yourselves treasures on earth, where moth and rust consume and where thieves break in and steal; but store up for yourselves treasures in heaven . . . for where your treasure is, there your heart will be also" (Matthew 6:19-21). The treasures we store up in heaven will never leave us feeling disappointed, whereas earthly treasures often do.

You may be wondering. In the previous chapter, I mentioned that I was thinking about buying a new car. Well, I did make that purchase and, as I always do, I bought one of the simplest and most inexpensive makes and models I could find. Power windows and power doors were deliberately rejected. I have owned a lot of new cars through the years. They have been useful and, with one notable exception, have brought me pleasure—but none has ever made me feel any happier. Even the most expensive car available could never earn me any "happiness points." I am also glad to say that I have never been in love with a car, as so many people seem to be. I am almost sure that there will be no automobiles in heaven!

Perhaps the search for happiness needs to be more of an internal than an external quest. That sounds promising—but let's go slowly and try to think this through. When we begin to focus on the inward aspects of happiness there are significant dangers to recognize and address. These may not be immediately apparent.

Here is one thing that causes me great concern. Could it be that *selfishness* is a real danger, almost an intrinsic risk, in any pursuit of happiness? That idea demands our most careful consideration. The other paths in search of worth that we have explored thus far—wealth, knowledge, fame, and power—have, at least to some degree, an *outward* orientation. They equip persons with resources and skills that can, if used well, help and bless other persons.

The search for worth through happiness, although usually sought in outward ways, actually tends to look *inward*, to focus on self. What makes *me* happy? "All *I* want is *just to be happy*." If we *really* mean that (and upon reflection most of us might want to disclaim that we do), then we are on a truly dangerous path. One thing for sure—this kind of concentration on self can *never* make us worth more than a hill of beans. There is nothing as small and insignificant as an individual who focuses primarily on self.

At this point, some readers who are pursuing happiness may want to object and insist that what makes them happy is the bringing of happiness into the life of others. Very good—but I would like to raise this question for you to consider: What is your *primary* motivation? Whose happiness are you really focused on? I have known some persons who claim that their most important goal in life is to make others happy, and they appear to be quite sincere. On closer examination, however, it becomes apparent that what they really want most is to gain happiness for themselves.

Let me illustrate by using a fictional character, once more drawing from the fascinating world of Christie. Miss Hartnell was a neighbor of the amateur, but enormously successful sleuth, Jane Marple. Miss Hartnell was a jolly woman, active in her church, who considered that her special calling in life was to minister to the Poor. She invested a lot of her time and energy in this ministry and expected to derive much joy from her work.

Unfortunately, she was actually much dreaded and detested by the Poor, and they did not want her in their homes! The truth was that Miss Hartnell had her own agenda, and although she tried diligently to minister to the needy, she did not really understand them. She had more concern for achieving her own happiness than she had compassion for those whom she tried to assist. Her "ministry" also caused the vicar of her church a lot of grief as he sought to respond to many complaints—from both sides!

This example is, of course, rather extreme (although I have known a few persons in real life who seem to follow the pattern of Miss Hartnell rather closely). Her story introduces this important principle. When you and I attempt to bring happiness to others—either in the course of our work or as just a part of everyday life—it is helpful to analyze our motivation. *The happiness that we can rightly accept and enjoy in such cases should be a BY-PRODUCT and never a planned primary result.*

Happy Are Those . . .

As I talk with persons about happiness, four words seem to occur more often than any others. These words embrace concepts that many people consider important in their struggle to define what it is that makes them happy. There are other words, of course, but these four, in my experience, have been mentioned most frequently. The first two are commonly included in dictionary definitions of "happiness," as noted previously.

The first word is *pleasure*. Life to be happy requires, many would say, a good helping of pleasure—and they pursue this avidly, sometimes meeting success and sometimes failure. There is one place, however, where pleasure can always be found. Hear these good words from an ancient and wise Psalmist. They have been authenticated through the centuries.

"You will show me the path that leads to life; your presence fills me with joy and brings me pleasure forever"

(Psalm 16:11, Today's English Version). God wants his children to have true and lasting pleasure—and not to be people who always seem to be walking around with grim, unhappy faces, refusing to laugh or even smile. At the risk of seeming irreverent, and being aware that life is not all "fun and games," I imagine there are times when God says to us, if we have ears to hear, "Lighten up a little! When you walk with ME you will have pleasure. Don't be afraid to let it show."

The second word is *joy*—also mentioned in the verse quoted above. This word resists all attempts to define it fully. I believe the chief reason for this is that no one can experience the fullness of joy while on earth—that is reserved for heaven. As C.S. Lewis states beautifully in *Letters to Malcolm*, "Joy is the serious business of Heaven." For the present, you and I can have only a taste of joy, an intense blend of delight, wonder, gladness, and all else that makes us feel truly good. Just a taste now—but one day a full glass of joy can be ours, a glass that will never become empty.

In the previous chapter, I referred to the fruit of the Spirit as presented in Galatians 5:22-23. Joy is the second fruit listed, and is produced in the life of a true child of God by the Holy Spirit. I am quite sure that there is no other source of authentic joy. Be aware, of this, however. There are many false advertisers trying to market "joy" who are vying for our attention. Let's just ignore them—and make them unhappy!

The third word that I want to mention is *contentment.* Over and over, people have told me that they just cannot be happy unless they are contented. Yes, but what do we insist on having in our life in order to be contented? There are so many different ways that this can be approached.

Are we talking about acquisitions of various types from the outside—possessions, fame, and the like—or qualities of life developed within? What does it take to make us content?

The Apostle Paul once observed, "I have learned to be content with whatever I have" (Philippians 4:11b). Regardless of inward and outward circumstances—"good" or "bad"—Paul had learned to be satisfied, and he knew that God would provide him all the strength he needed. On those occasions when Paul experienced serious external difficulties, and also when he was beset with strong internal fears, he was encouraged by God, who was his unfailing source of joy (see 2 Corinthians 7:5-7). Notice that his confidence and his ability to cope were *learned*—not just hoped for, or dreamed into existence. It was probably a difficult lesson for Paul, but he was a good student, and God was his Teacher. He will also teach us.

Lastly, but perhaps expressed most often, and with greatest fervor, people tell me that they want *peace*. Happiness, it seems, cannot exist in a person in the absence of peace. Unfortunately, the lack of peace seems all too common. Anxiety and distress rob many of us of the happiness that we work so diligently to find and enjoy. They thwart our strategy at every turn. We appear to live in an increasingly anxious time, and no relief is in sight. Is there any antidote? Any solution we can trust?

Let's take one last glance at Careers. In that game, no place is made for religious faith and practice as part of any of the avenues leading to success, including that of happiness. For the person seeking happiness in real life, and especially for the one wanting peace, to factor God out of the equation is a tragic error with horrific consequences. Readers familiar with the Bible will know that the theme of peace runs throughout its pages. Let's look at just a few of the important things that Scripture has to say about peace.

The prophet Isaiah, speaking to God, was convinced of this important truth: "Those of a steadfast mind you keep in peace—in peace because they trust in you" (Isaiah 26:3). The same prophet looked forward to the day when a "Prince of Peace" would come (Isaiah 9:6). Centuries passed, and then a baby who was given the name of Jesus was born, and Isaiah's dream was realized. On that night, we are told that a multitude of angels sang "Glory to God in the highest, and on earth peace, good will toward men" (Luke 2:14, King James Version).

Jesus, however, was not welcomed by all of earth's people. He, himself, recognized that he would at times be a divisive influence. His presence and his call for people to make decisions that are of utmost importance could actually shatter what seemed to be peace, even within families. Hear his solemn words: "Do you think that I have come to bring peace to the earth? No, I tell you, but rather division" (Luke 12:51)! Jesus goes on to add that the members of households will be divided, even disrupting relationships between parents and children.

The most important kind of peace, the only true and lasting peace, is that which can exist between God and those who choose to make him their Lord. Now, hear these words of Jesus, spoken to his disciples on the night before his crucifixion: "Peace I leave with you; my peace I give to you. I do not give to you as the world gives. Do not let your hearts be troubled, and do not let them be afraid" (John 14:27).

Here is another word from Scripture about peace. The Apostle Paul led what was in many ways a difficult and turbulent life. He learned, however, that real peace could be found through faith in God. Growing out of his own personal experiences, he could reassure Christians at the church in Philippi (and all others, then and now) with these words: "The peace of God, which surpasses all understanding, will guard your hearts and your minds in Christ Jesus" (Philippians 4:7). To which I would like to say, "Amen!"

Throughout this chapter, we have been plagued by our inability to fully define what makes us happy. Even those of us who seem to have a reasonably clear idea of what *we* want in *our* "happiness package" have to admit that we change our minds from time to time. Also, we are disappointed in some of our acquisitions, and tire quickly of others. Obtaining—and retaining—happiness seems to be a very tricky and precarious project. I believe a look at some additional words from Scripture concerning happiness will be exceedingly helpful.

First, here are some wise words from the book of Psalms: "Happy is everyone who fears the Lord, who walks in his ways. You shall eat the fruit of the labor of your hands; you shall be happy, and it shall go well with you" (Psalm 128:1-2). Now, let's turn to some very famous words in the New Testament.

At the beginning of chapter five of the Gospel of Matthew, one finds a series of short utterances by Jesus that have come to be known as The Beatitudes. They form an introduction to what is often called The Sermon on the Mount. Many of you are probably already quite familiar with these famous sayings, each beginning with the word "Blessed." As a reminder, the first Beatitude reads: "Blessed are the poor in spirit, for theirs is the kingdom of heaven" (Matthew 5:3). "Poor in spirit" means one who is not proud and who recognizes his or her own spiritual poverty.

Now, here is something that I find very interesting. The Greek word usually translated "Blessed" (*makarias*) can just as correctly be translated "Happy," and this is done in some modern versions of Scripture. For example, The Living Bible and also Today's English Version each choose the word "Happy." Here we have a fascinating opportunity to see human happiness from God's perspective—and only he knows what can bring us true and lasting happiness. I strongly urge you to read, carefully and prayerfully, Matthew 5:1-12, substituting "Happy" for "Blessed" as needed. This is a spiritual exercise that will probably call most of us to revise our concept of the nature of happiness.

In the Balance

Remember that our goal is to find a way to acquire personal worth. The time has come for us to weigh the results of our search for worth through the achievement of happiness. There is no doubt that the various components of happiness as ordinarily understood can sometimes enrich our lives and make them more pleasant and enjoyable. I do not find any evidence, however, that the possession of this type of happiness results in our becoming persons of worth. In fact, the search for happiness—even if we are successful—may indeed subtract from whatever worth we might already have.

A "hill of beans" with lots of toys is still a hill of beans, and maybe not a very healthy one at that! "Happiness" gained at the expense of others will ultimately prove to be false and will dwindle away. "Happiness" built on selfishness cannot endure for very long. The more determined we are in our pursuit of happiness, the more it becomes obvious that the whole venture is a will-o'-the-wisp.

Worth will never be found by chasing happiness.

Could it be, however, that persons who already have worth, and who recognize its presence, will be happy? I believe so. They will be happy as God defines happiness. That is all that really matters—now and later. But—how do *I* find this kind of worth? I want so much to be a worthy person, but the search has been long and difficult, and I am becoming confused and bewildered. Who *am* I? Am I worth anything to anyone—or am I just a useless nobody? Where do I go from here?

Chapter Six

A Name for a "Nobody"

The slender, mentally confused fifteen-year-old boy, responding with hesitation and bewilderment to a request for his name, replied "I don't know who I am; I'm jest a nobody. Nobody can't have no name, can he?" The boy's name is actually Pete, and he is a character in one of the most beautiful and powerful stories ever written. Harold Bell Wright's classic novel, *The Shepherd of the Hills*, which was first published in 1907, has been read and loved by millions of people throughout the world. I discovered it early in life since I grew up less than thirty miles from the story's setting in the Ozark Hills of Missouri. I still consider "Ozarkian" language my native tongue!—but my computer doesn't like it at all!!

In the Introduction to his book, Wright—referring to the story he is about to tell—says this: "In the story, it all happened in the Ozark Mountains, many miles from what we of the city call civilization. In life, it has all happened many, many times before, in many, many places." It is certainly true that Pete's dilemma, one part of the story, has been experienced in real life by many people in many places, and it continues to be a serious problem today. This lament is still being raised by a multitude of folks: "I'm jest a nobody. I don't know what my name is. Can 'nobody' even have a name?"

In biblical times, one's name was considered to be quite important. The essence of persons, their most basic identity, was embodied in the name by which they were known. When a significant change occurred in the character of a person, he or she was often given a new name. Names meant something back in those days—but could a name be given to a "nobody"?

On one occasion, Job, who was sorely beset by many difficulties, lashed out bitterly at a group of men whom he considered to be worn out and useless. He called them "a worthless bunch of nameless nobodies" (Job 30:8, Today's English Version). I cannot imagine words more stinging! Let's look closely at his statement, beginning at the end and working back to the beginning.

As far as Job was concerned, these men were just plain *nobodies*—and since they were nobodies they are said to be *nameless*. Apparently Job would agree with Pete that you can't have a name if you are a nobody. Now, notice this: In the thinking of Job, if you are a nameless nobody you are also *worthless*. Many people today feel worthless and they struggle to find and establish a basic identity—one that they hope will be worth more than a hill of beans.

We have been thinking together about various ways people commonly seek worth, but what we have found has not been very encouraging. Perhaps we have been going about this project backwards. Could it be that our basic premise and orientation have been wrong? Later in this chapter, we will revisit a young man who now knows that his name is Pete, and who can say with confidence, "I ain't nobody no more." Maybe . . . maybe . . . just maybe he will provide us with a useful clue to help us in our search for worth. We can certainly use his assistance. But first it will be of value to consider *why* it is that so many people feel worthless.

Beginning Under a Cloud

During the time I was a practicing pediatrician, I had the great privilege of meeting many babies either at the time of their birth or within a few hours thereafter. I always considered it to be a significant and awe-inspiring moment. I knew that a complex array of genetic and environmental factors were already at work, shaping the newborn into the person he or she presently was and would become. Based on the knowledge and information that I possessed, I was happy for some and worried about others—but I could never know for sure how things would ultimately work out for any of them.

Because of differences in their temperament and disposition, which appear to be present in some degree from the beginning, infants and children often respond in quite different ways to similar experiences encountered in nearly identical environments. While some thrive even under cloudy and threatening skies, others are harmed and warped by the storms that come their way. Let's consider some of the challenges infants, children, and youths might confront that could cause them to have doubts about their self-worth.

Perhaps we should begin with the obvious. Any physical defect, congenital or acquired, that affects the appearance and/or the function of the body can have a significant impact on one's self-image. In some cases, such persons become the target of much unkind and unwelcome attention. Unfortunately, bullies of the spirit continue to be all too common. Such bullies have their own set of problems which may be quite complex and which should not be ignored.

Parents, teachers, and other significant adults in a child's life should work together to help and encourage the one with a physical defect, as well as the bully who has other, less visible flaws, and endeavor to mitigate all negative influences. More resources to aid such persons are available now than in earlier generations, and no avenues of legitimate medical, surgical, social, and psychological help should be left unexplored.

Persons whose body is not "perfect" should still be able to feel good about themselves, and we need to help them be able to do so. For six years, I worked part time as the Pediatric Consultant for the Commission for Handicapped Children of the state of Kentucky. My heart was warmed by the attitude of many youngsters who remained optimistic and positive despite their struggle with significant physical problems. Children tend to have an amazing resiliency. Tragically, however, there are some who come to harbor grave doubts about their self-worth. This need not be so.

Let's broaden our scope now to include all children. A good place to begin is with a consideration of the child's home environment, for it is especially there that self-esteem and long-lasting concepts of worth are developed. Numerous things work together to shape a youngster's attitude toward self. Three of the most important are acceptance, affection, and affirmation. *Acceptance* means that the child is assured that he or she is truly wanted and will be provided security. *Affection* establishes an environment of love that is essential for healthy physical, mental, and emotional growth and development. *Affirmation* gives a child direct and definite reassurance that he or she does have value and worth.

We all know, however, that not every child is blessed with a positive home environment. Acceptance, affection, and affirmation are often withheld and a child can be terribly neglected—or even become the target of much that is downright negative and hurtful. Verbal, emotional, and physical abuse of children is an awful scourge in too many homes. As odd as it might seem, many abused children form the idea that they actually deserve such mistreatment. This *totally erroneous belief* can persist into adulthood and can be very difficult to dislodge. It is easy to see, I believe, how destructive this can be to a person's concept of self-worth.

Then there is the old and well-known phenomenon of sibling rivalry, based in one way or another on comparison and competition among the children in a home. Who is the prettiest . . . the smartest . . . the most talented? Am I the "Ugly Duckling" . . . the dunce . . . the klutz? Do my parents love my brother and sister more than they do me? Children are usually able to work through these issues satisfactorily and without too many residual scars—but it is not always so. In some instances, a child's self-image is marred, with long-lasting results. Jealousy is always ugly—it disturbs relationships and it crushes feelings of confidence and worth.

Now for a change of scene. Entering school ushers one onto a larger stage. Some issues that have been wrestled with at home may become even more troublesome, and new ones are encountered. School years can be immensely enjoyable and rewarding for some children and youths—for others that time may seem very much like a bit of hell here on earth (especially for those who are victims of others who tease and bully). Without any doubt, experiences at school have a huge influence on an individual's development and understanding of personal worth. Let's consider a few of the important areas where problems can occur.

Social issues of various types are very disturbing to some students. A child who belongs to a minority group may find it difficult to adjust to a classroom setting, especially if there are associated factors such as poverty, or perhaps a language barrier. Peer pressure is usually immense, and *anything* that makes it more difficult for a child to "fit in" can cause much doubt and frustration. Children can be quite cruel to one another at times, and insults suffered can be harbored and resented throughout a person's lifetime. This is particularly apt to happen when the child who encounters unkindness at school has a less than satisfactory home environment.

Let's get more personal and inject ourselves into this discussion—if we dare to do so! Think back to your own years in grade school and high school. Can you remember perhaps as many as five times when you were made to feel less than adequate? How much did it hurt then? Does it still bother you, or can you now look back and laugh about those times? What did you do to "get over" it? (If you have matters that still cause you a lot of pain, you might want to read my book *Long Shadows: Redeeming the Past*.)

I would like to share one of my (recurrent) experiences with you. This is *my* story, but it is also one that has "happened many, many times in many, many places." Some schools have now taken measures to prevent the kind of trauma that I will describe. I am very glad that this is so.

Most of the students in my grade school looked forward eagerly to the twenty-minutes recesses we were given twice a day. I, however, often dreaded those times because they all too frequently included a quick game of softball. Two of our athletic-type boys would be designated captains and they would take turns picking the members for their team. I probably would have been a pretty good player except for three things—I could not hit the ball, nor throw the ball, nor catch the ball! Since standards were high (!), it was a foregone conclusion that I would always be chosen last (and with reluctance). Fortunately, I was never teased or belittled about my total ineptitude as a softball player. I knew, and the other kids knew, that recesses were over quickly. Soon we would be back in the classroom where *I* was an undisputed "captain"—and in those days academic achievement was respected and honored by one's fellow students. It is always good when you have strengths to offset your weaknesses. *But what about those who are not so fortunate?* I was aware of some kids who received very little affirmation at school—and probably even less at home.

While inferiority complexes may most often be conceived at home, they have a way of being born at school. Why do so many folks wonder if they are worth a hill of beans? Those crippling doubts often date back to school days. Schools are of tremendous importance, and education is a treasure—but for all too many people the years of formal schooling are endured with difficulty and result in long-remembered pain. Clouds from the past linger into the present, and the pitter-patter of their rain seems to whisper, "You aren't worth very much."

Poor Return on Investments

Sooner or later, we complete our formal schooling, which might include attendance at an institution of higher education, and we are thrust into what is often called "the real world." I have always disliked that phrase and consider it simplistic and misleading. Some of my most "real" times were found in schools, and I have had far too many "unreal" experiences outside of academia. I suspect that is also true for some of you who are reading this.

Be that as it may, we do reach the stage where we are expected to find a job, become self-supporting, and perhaps establish a family. In previous chapters, we have examined several different routes people have traditionally taken in order to achieve success and demonstrate their worth. Much energy and time is spent chasing our dreams—but the return on our investment is sometimes most disappointing.

Somewhere along the way, many of us begin to realize, probably with alarm and dismay, that our career is not going nearly as well as we had hoped it would. Failures are encountered that cause great discouragement. Perhaps it is difficulty in securing work that we really like . . . or the loss of one or more jobs . . . or being passed over repeatedly for a promotion . . . or a distinctly unfriendly workplace. Maybe it is the dawning realization that our expectations have been set too high and that we have over-estimated our abilities. Others about us appear to be doing far better than we—and suddenly we are seized with doubt and despair.

"Might as well face it," we say to our self, "I'm just not worth very much." The prospect of a lifetime of mediocrity or even failure is not easy to face. For some of us, difficulties at work are compounded by other factors, such as marital problems, mounting debts, or the onset of a chronic illness. At this point, some of us might well be tempted to say, "My name—if I have one—is FAILURE."

Failures at work can definitely cause almost anyone to

suffer a loss of self-esteem. Strangely enough, however, so can success. In fact, "success" can be more destructive than the corrosive effects of failure to a person's feeling of worth. The phenomenon of "success failure" is commonplace and occurs in at least two guises. We need to be aware of these and respond in appropriate ways when necessary.

J. B. Phillips, who died in 1982, was a brilliant author and talented translator of Scripture. He became a very famous man, one that I greatly admired and appreciated. At the beginning of his autobiography, *The Price of Success*, Phillips writes that he had long been "aware of the dangers of sudden wealth and I took some severe measures to make sure that, although comfortable, I should never be rich." C. S. Lewis had similar thoughts, and both of these men refused to accept royalties from several of their books. (On a *much* smaller scale, I, too, have refused to make a profit on any of my books.)

Phillips goes on to add these perceptive words: "I was not nearly so aware of the dangers of success. The subtle corrosion of character, the unconscious changing of values and the secret monstrous growth of a vastly inflated idea of myself seeped slowly into me." This is one of the ways that "success failures" can occur, and many persons are unaware of the danger and are also oblivious to this failure in their life when it occurs.

Persons who have achieved success in one or more of the ways we have looked at in earlier chapters are prone to develop some ugly and serious flaws of character. They may succeed gloriously in their career and fail miserably as a decent human being. As Phillips noted, the development of these flaws is often so subtle that they tend to slip in unawares. Other people usually notice these defects long before the affected person becomes aware of their presence (if he or she *ever* does).

Among these ugly "warts" are such things as conceit, arrogance, rudeness, pride, smugness, and selfishness. These lead to various other types of unattractive attitudes and behavior. For example, persons who are "success failures" may lose touch with the way the majority of people think and live. These "elite" ones may begin to view "commoners" as being important only to the extent that they can contribute, with admiration and applause, to their own career and happiness. Their view of what has true value can easily become twisted and warped.

Along with this, some can exhibit a decided tendency to feel that they are not subject to the same rules, regulations, and expectations that apply to the masses. They often feel "above" those around them. An exaggerated concept of their own importance leads them to expect and demand special and favored treatment wherever they go—and they can become outraged if their "royal" status is not recognized and honored.

As I wrote these last few paragraphs, I was thinking of several specific persons! I imagine that my words also call a number of people to your mind. This category of "success failure" is large and growing. These unfortunate folks, when and if they become aware of their problem, would be wise to ask themselves this sober question: "Am I truly successful if I have failed so dismally to achieve the status of a worthy human being?" The correct answer is surely obvious.

There is another large group of "success failures." I alluded to these folks briefly in chapter five and am referring to those who have been quite successful in achieving their goals, only to be disillusioned with the results. They may feel like the ancient "wise" man who had worked hard and had acquired much knowledge, wealth, fame, and power—only to find no satisfaction, and he concluded that his endeavor was "worthless and the chasing of the unattainable" (Ecclesiastes 2:17b, My translation). Many people have found that the return on their investments has been excellent in some respects—but grossly lacking in matters of real importance.

A change in career, if still possible, is unlikely to bring much satisfaction unless attention is first given to matters of more fundamental importance. Persons in this category of "success failure" should seek to profit from what they have learned, and give careful and thoughtful consideration to what success really means. Surely, its primary ingredients should not be misery, depression, and a feeling of being a failure and a "nobody." A bit later, we will see how Pete, one of the world's "little people," found real success—and how we can do the same.

Is This the Best?

"Grow old along with me! The best is yet to be, the last of life, for which the first was made." These words of Robert Browning, found in "Rabbi Ben Ezra," have encouraged thousands of persons in their journey through life. I strongly suspect, however, that they have puzzled and disappointed thousands of others—for it is among the elderly that feelings of worthlessness are perhaps most prevalent. Their response to Browning might be: "Is this the best? Really? Something seems to have gone dreadfully wrong." Such attitudes have a history and are shaped by a host of factors.

Culture is one of the primary players in determining

the plight of older persons. The way elderly folks are regarded by society has vast importance in the shaping of the quality of life these persons will have. In those cultures where older people are respected—even honored and revered—the later years of their life can be filled with happiness and satisfaction. When their value and importance is acknowledged, the elderly also have an opportunity to contribute their wise thoughts and utilize their many gifts for the enrichment of the younger generations.

In those places where there is an overemphasis on being young—and where the elderly are regarded by society as "has-beens" and no longer of value—a person's later years can be long, lonely, and devoid of the support that is needed to sustain them during this "best" part of their life. In my country, the United States, a correction in orientation is needed. This may be coming because an increasingly large segment of the population is comprised of the elderly. They cannot and will not be ignored. Society should recognize the contributions and worth of every age group, including the elderly, and address their specific needs in a comprehensive way.

Remember, though, that *you and I* are part of "society," and should not shirk our individual responsibility to older folks. As we have opportunity, let's *encourage* elderly persons, and help them to understand that it is *all right* to be old—no apologies needed! Some of us, of course, will be speaking to ourselves! We all need to work to help create a climate in which the elderly are appreciated and respected.

The family, however, is the principal unit that determines how satisfactory the later years of an individual are apt to be. When I was a child growing up in a large family in the Ozarks, I was taught by word and example that we had a life-long commitment to look out for one another.

That principle is a good one, but there are far too many persons who reach advanced age without having this kind of support. The reasons are multiple.

Some older folks simply do not have much or any family remaining, or no members that are willing to help, and they find themselves on their own. This can easily lead to fear and depression—and to a sense that they have outlived any possibility of being considered a person of worth to anyone. All that remains, they may think, is to wait for the "end"—feeling useless and forgotten. In reality, they are never useless, but they may indeed be forgotten by most.

In addition to having a lack of close family, some persons reach the advanced age when almost no one around them is left who can remember with them those long-ago days of their youth. Miss Jane Marple, the fictional solver of complex mysteries, whom I have mentioned previously, felt this keenly. With reference to past pleasures she had enjoyed, we find these wistful words in Christie's *At Bertram's Hotel*: "If you could find someone to remember them with, that was indeed happiness. Nowadays that was not easy to do; she had outlived most of her contemporaries." Many older people in real life understand these words perfectly well—and it hurts a lot.

Fortunately for herself, Miss Marple was kept exceptionally busy bringing murderers to justice, and modestly accepting the applause and appreciation of a grateful public—and also experiencing a great inner satisfaction. She was still useful! In real life, however, such rewards are rare. Many of the very old persons whom I know tend to live with memories that are difficult to share with others with any hope of these being truly appreciated. Memories, however, if they are good ones, can still bring pleasure even if they cannot be fully understood by others.

We have glanced very briefly at the role of society and the place of the family in aiding elderly individuals to have and maintain a healthy sense of self-esteem. Ultimately, however, much will rest directly on the personal inner resources of each older man and woman. If we find ourselves wondering what a person (let's include ourselves) will be like in old age, a useful clue is at hand.

Those persons who are presently hopeful, optimistic, adaptable, resourceful, generous in spirit, interested in the world about them, and who have a good sense of humor, will *usually* carry these valuable traits into their old age. The prevention of many of the undesirable characteristics exhibited by some older folks should be directed toward the discovery and correction of unhealthy attitudes and practices *before* the "golden years" are entered.

There are, of course, some persons who develop serious health problems, including various types of dementia, in later life. The first evidence of these may be mood and personality changes. These folks deserve our love, respect, and appropriate care. All available resources should be used in their support. One very important resource that I have not yet mentioned, but one that can be of tremendous value for all persons—not just those who are old, ill, and perhaps confused—is the church. Blessed indeed are the men and women who have the loving congregation of a local church available to encourage and sustain them in all the stages of life.

Elderly persons do, indeed, face numerous challenges and some of these dear folks may legitimately wonder about the validity of Browning's words. Many rise to these challenges and enjoy their later years. Others, however, see the reservoir of their self-esteem draining away—until it runs dry. These persons may feel a bit like Job, who at one point in his life uttered these forlorn words, "My days are swifter than a weaver's shuttle, and come to their end without hope" (Job 7:6). But, do you know what happened? Job had an encounter with God—and everything changed for the better. The same thing can happen to any of us.

At this point, I would like to make a suggestion. For additional reading on aging, I recommend the chapter on this topic in my book, *Less Than a Mile*. I try to present a balanced view of the elderly—emphasizing strengths, pointing out "uglies" of attitude and practice that some develop, and offering a few "prescriptions" that should be beneficial. I believe that you will find it of interest. For now, however, let's turn our full attention elsewhere—let's listen to a still small voice that has a very important message for each of us.

A Still Small Voice

Years ago, my teenage son, Doug, and I were hiking together in the Mojave Desert. Suddenly he stopped and said, "Listen, Dad." We both stood still for a few moments, and then I said, "I don't hear anything." "Yes," he replied, "isn't it wonderful?" He was correct. The desert lay resting in the hot mid-afternoon sun. Birds were quiet. No planes were in the sky. No sounds reached us from the faraway and little-traveled road. We had found an oasis of quietness where, at least for a time, it was totally silent. Yes, it was a wonderful and rare experience in what continues to become an increasingly noisy world.

In *The Screwtape Letters* by C. S. Lewis, we can read the advice and counsel that a senior devil named Screwtape gives to his nephew, a junior devil named Wormwood. At one point, Screwtape mentions how much Satan hates silence—and loves noise. Speaking for his Father Below, Screwtape says: "We will make the whole universe a noise in the end. We have already made great strides in this direction as regards Earth." Yes, that is lamentably true. Personally, I hate noise—and I call on all Christians to fight actively against this tool of the Devil! In a quieter world, we will be able to better hear that which is *important*—that which has *worth*.

In word often quoted from another C. S. Lewis book, *The Problem of Pain*, Lewis writes "God whispers to us in our pleasures, speaks in our conscience, but shouts in our pain; it is His megaphone to rouse a deaf world." Perhaps once in a while God does shout —but I believe he conducts *most* of his conversations with us in a whisper, and we must be quiet in order to hear what he says.

The Psalmist has said, "Be still, and know that I am God" (Psalm 46:10a). I am reminded of the experience of the prophet Elijah, who fled to a remote place of hiding to escape the wrath of the wicked queen, Jezebel. Well, Jezebel did not find Elijah, but God did. When God drew near to Elijah, there was a strong wind, then an earthquake, and then a fire—but God did not speak to the prophet in any of these ways. Finally, there was "a sound of sheer silence" (1 Kings 19:12b) and in that absolute silence Elijah clearly heard the voice of God speaking to him. That can be our experience also, if we will wait and listen for God—for when we do, we will hear his voice.

God whispers something into our ear, and in dazed amazement our ensuing conversation with God might go something like this. "*I* am a person of worth?" "Yes." I *am* a person of worth?" "Yes." I am a person of *worth*" "Yes." "*I am already a person of worth*?" "Yes, child. You have been all the time that you were feverishly seeking worth in this way and that." That is the glorious reality that God wants us to embrace—and to understand more fully.

I am aware, however, that some of you who are reading this may find it difficult to believe that God cares anything about you. Perhaps you have tried and have been unable to find him. Your inability to do so may suggest to you that you have no worth, and you could even be angry with yourself and with God because of your failure. Let's look at this from two different angles that share a common theme. First, hear these good words from Jesus: "So I say to you, Ask, and it will be given you; knock, and the door will be opened for you. . . . everyone who searches finds, and for everyone who knocks, the door will be opened" (Luke 11:9, 10b). Sometimes our own problems get in the way of our finding God—but we should definitely keep on knocking!

There is, however, another side of this picture to consider. The members of the first-century church at Laodicea had become lukewarm in their relationship with God and had drifted far away from him. Jesus said to them: "Listen! I am standing at the door, knocking: if you hear my voice and open the door, I will come in to you and eat with you and you with me" (Revelation 3:20). Jesus stands at the door of many hearts today and wants to come in. Listen carefully—and when you hear him knocking, throw the door wide open! You do *not* have to do any "house cleaning" first!

Pete was an illegitimate and mentally confused child whose young mother died when he was born. His father had long fled the area by the time of Pete's birth, but later he returned and established a relationship with the boy. Pete did not know that the man who treated him so kindly was actually his father. He did, however, know one thing—when he was in the presence of this one who seemed to be like God to him, he no longer felt like a "nobody." He was a "somebody" whose name was Pete—such was the power of his father's influence on him

Such a simple, but profound truth! The implications transcend this earth. When you and I come into the presence of our heavenly Father, bringing with us all of our hurts, weaknesses, and failures, we *know* that we are not meant to be a "nobody." We are enfolded in the cloak of our Father's love and made to understand that we have worth—for we, all of us, have been created in the image of God.

Chapter Seven

In the Image of God

Long ago, a Hebrew Psalmist stood under a starry sky and was overcome with awe as he marveled at the greatness of God as seen in the magnificence of his creation. He became acutely aware of his own insignificance and smallness, and was moved to say to God, "What are human beings that you are mindful of them, mortals that you care for them? Yet you have made them a little lower than God, and crowned them with glory and honor" (Psalm 8:4-5). A footnote added to the word "God" by the translator indicates that the enigmatic Hebrew words could be translated in other ways.

Older English versions of the Bible usually read, "a little lower than the angels." Most modern translators have abandoned this practice—and for good reasons. "Angels" is not a satisfactory translation either linguistically (the Hebrew word for "angel" is not present) or theologically (human beings are not a lower form of creation than angels). What, then, would be a reasonable translation?

Among the various choices found in more recent English translations of the Bible, one finds such words as "God," "a god," "heavenly beings," "divine," and "Yourself." Because of its compatibility with the underlying Hebrew text, and also its readability, I like the New

Living Translation, which reads "For you made us only a little lower than God, and you crowned us with glory and honor."

Whatever choice of words is made, the message is quite clear. As difficult as it was for the Psalmist (and us) to understand, human beings are very special indeed! But how in the world is that possible? It seems to be almost incomprehensible. During my six summers digging in Israel as a member of The Joint Archaeological Expedition to Tell el-Hesi, I often stood under a *really dark* nighttime sky (impossible to find near my home) and looked up—and could understand how the Psalmist from long ago must have felt.

I think of Psalm 8 as the "Little Person, Big Person" Psalm. Any adequate theology must make allowance for both the littleness of human beings and also their greatness. To begin to understand this paradox, we must go back to the beginning. Only from that perspective can we hope to see things in their proper balance.

A Special Creation

Let's begin by looking at three verses from Scripture. They will be familiar to many of you.

"In the beginning God created the heavens and the earth" (Genesis 1:1, New American Standard Bible).

". . . God created humankind in his image, in the image of God he created them; male and female he created them" (Genesis 1:27).

"God saw everything that he had made, and indeed, it was very good" (Genesis 1:31a).

The Bible in numerous places affirms that the One who is eternal created all that exists—the cosmos and everything that it contains. In the first chapter of Genesis, God's creative work is portrayed as occurring over a period of time, with human beings created last. Men and women were created to complement one another and to be fully equal. Their special status is clearly indicated by the fact that they were created *in the image of God*. This is a truly amazing reality—but what does it mean?

First, I believe the most important aspect of being made in God's image is that, in all of God's creation, only human beings have the opportunity to enter fully into a close, personal, reciprocal relationship with the Living God. As sexual beings, men and women are created to live in community with one another; as persons created in the image of God they are meant to live in fellowship with their Creator. The Bible uses several different metaphors to describe the relationship between God and human beings. The most meaningful of these is parent-child. We are the children of God—and, as such, we have immense worth!

Also, there are other important factors to consider. God gives to you and me, as ones created in his image, the freedom to choose. In fact, he insists that we make our own choices—he will not make our decisions for us. We even have the freedom to disobey God. This has, of course, led to all kinds of problems. Freedom of choice, however, is an *intrinsic* element of "image of God."

Along with items already mentioned, we also should recognize other attributes that we have, at least in some measure, as persons created in our Heavenly Father's image. I think of such things as self-awareness, intelligence, the capacity to love, emotions, and creativity. God has equipped us with what we need to lead the kind of life he wants his children to have.

Then, there is the element of authority. God chose to assign us important duties. He said that we are to "fill the earth and subdue it; and have dominion over the fish of the sea and over the birds of the air and over every living thing that moves on the earth" (Genesis 1:28). Needless to say, none of this authority is to be exercised in a careless or ruthless fashion. We are strictly accountable to God for the way we carry out his directions—but there is great joy in using our abilities and gifts to help him accomplish his purposes.

We must not miss the significance of Genesis 1:31a. As God completed each phase of his creative work, he declared it to be "good." And at the end of this work, culminating with the creation of human life, he pronounced all of it to be "very good." This is God's way of saying that everything turned out to be exactly as he intended. There were no "manufacturing errors"! No recalls were necessary!

As we reflect on these wonders, I believe it should be abundantly clear to all of us that you and I have indeed been created to be very special persons. God himself has indelibly stamped each one of us with the word "*worth.*" No one should doubt his judgment, for he alone is able to impart and define worth. We did nothing to merit or earn this commendation—it is the free gift of God.

At this point, however, it is essential that we understand one thing thoroughly. God is the Creator—we are the ones created. Confusion in this matter has led to many problems. I will mention two. First, we must accept the truth that we were created to be human beings—not God. Though created in his image, we are exceedingly small when compared with the Divine One. Any endeavor we might undertake to elevate ourselves to the stature of God will end in disaster. We will return to this idea soon.

Second, as many have observed, God created us in *his* image—and ever since that time we have been busy trying to create God in *our* image! Our concepts of him, conditioned by our own desires and limited understanding, are woefully inadequate. J. B. Phillips, mentioned in chapter six, wrote a Christian classic called *Your God is Too Small*, which I very highly recommend. In this small volume, Phillips discusses common and inadequate ideas of God that many of us have, and then he helps us to move on to a better understanding of the true nature of God.

We are made in the image of God! What exciting possibilities that promises! I surely do want to believe it is true, and I certainly don't want to doubt God's word. However . . . when I look closely and honestly at myself, I find tendencies and characteristics there that are definitely not part of the makeup of God. I am confused. How can I with my multiple flaws and deficiencies possibly be made in the image of God? Do you have similar thoughts about yourself? Something must have happened!

I seem to remember two old stories. One is about a tree and the other is about a tower. They are actually the same story in essence, just told in different ways. Their setting is the ancient Near East—but the events related have happened "many, many times in many, many places." To continue quoting from *The Shepherd of the Hills*, "The story, so very old, is still in the telling."

I Know What's Best For Me

"I know what's best for me." Those words, perhaps uttered with a note of defiance, are heard quite often. For example, they may be spoken by a child to a parent, a student to a teacher, a friend to a friend, or even a patient to a physician. Sometimes the speaker is correct—more often than not, however, he or she is quite mistaken. I have learned from personal experience and through observation of others that you and I tend to be badly misinformed about what is best for us—and when we speak those words to God we are *always* wrong.

The ludicrous idea that we know better than God what is best for us first surfaced in the beautiful Garden of Eden, the home of Adam and Eve. This couple, representative of earliest human life, enjoyed close fellowship with their Creator, and they were entrusted with the care of the Garden. There was, however, one tree in the midst of the Garden that was strictly off-limits. God warned that eating the fruit of that tree would be deadly. Let's take a close look at this special, symbolic tree.

My translation of Genesis 2:17a is quite literal and also reflects the punctuation supplied by Hebrew scribes. It reads this way (please note the commas): "Of the tree of knowledge, good and evil, you shall not eat." I prefer this to common translations that read, "the tree of the knowledge of good and evil," suggesting a wisdom given to the consumer of the fruit to make moral judgments. As generally recognized by students of Scripture, the meaning is much broader in scope—it refers to *all* knowledge, with no restrictions.

Only One person is "all-knowing," and he has established limits in the area of knowledge between himself and the rest of his creation. Omniscience would be a terribly perilous possession for any human being. The tree, therefore, was forbidden to Adam and Eve—not as a kind of test of obedience, but because the tree was dangerous and deadly.

The couple was well aware, however, of the attractiveness of the tree. The probable tastiness of its fruit, along with its hoped-for benefit of making them wise like God, fascinated them. Encouraged by personal evil from the outside, symbolized by a serpent, later to be understood as Satan, they succumbed to temptation and ate from the tree. The whole sordid story, familiar to many of you, is related in the third chapter of Genesis.

Gerhard von Rad, in volume one of his *Old Testament Theology*, summarizes the matter very well: "By endeavoring to enlarge his being on the godward side, and seeking a godlike intensification of his life beyond his creaturely limitations, that is, by wanting to be like God, man stepped out from the simplicity of obedience to God. He thereby forfeited life in the pleasant garden and close to God." Adam and Eve refused to accept responsibility for what they had done, and the consequences were immediate and immense.

The first of these mentioned is the couple's sudden awareness that they were naked. They became *ashamed* and quickly made for themselves garments of fig leaves (Genesis 3:7). Borrowing some of my own words from *Becoming One*, "The meaning is profound and has little to do with clothing (or the lack thereof) for the physical body. The picture, rather, is of a couple who initially had no secrets to hide, nothing to make them feel uncomfortable or guilty. They could be transparent and unafraid." Shame, however, drove a wedge between them—their close relationship was disrupted.

Next, there is the matter of fear. Now they are *afraid* to be in the presence of God (Genesis 3:8-10). A couple meant to live in a trusting and joyful relationship with their Creator became afraid to have him come near to them!

Estranged from one another and from God—what a tragedy! God had told them that if they ate from the forbidden tree they would die. Did that happen? Yes.

To be estranged from God is to be dead *spiritually*; before long Adam and Eve would also die *physically*. There was another special tree in the Garden that the couple would have had access to if they had remained obedient. Now, however, they found themselves driven from the Garden—and the way to the Tree of Life was blocked by a flaming sword (Genesis 3:24). Death reigned.

"I know what's best for me." Really? The story of Adam and Eve suggests otherwise. There is another thing that we don't want to miss. The rebellion in the Garden was no small matter—it had cosmic significance. Because of disobedience, the very ground was cursed (Genesis 3:17-18). *All* of God's creation would suffer because of the sin of its highest members. It seems clear that *all* sins are *big* sins. When persons sin, they become cosmic sinners!

Perhaps, however, human beings learned a lesson from that most painful and devastating episode with the tree. Maybe they would do better in the future. Surely they would now obey God. I go back in imagination to that early time to check on how things are going. What is that I see in the distance? I believe it looks like . . . yes . . . it looks like a tower. I wonder what it could be?

Readers who are familiar with the Bible will know that the history of human beings following their expulsion from their home in the Garden is full of bloodshed and violence. The picture grew darker and darker until a day came when God "saw that the wickedness of humankind was great in the earth, and that every inclination of the thoughts of their hearts was only evil continually" (Genesis 6:5). Judgment came in the form of a great flood that destroyed everyone except for Noah, a man faithful to God, and his immediate family. The earth was washed clean and the stage was set for a fresh start, a new beginning. It was a time to hope, and to make plans for a bright future.

When the flood was over, God established his covenant with Noah and his sons, and with their descendants. A beautiful bow graced the sky above them (Genesis 9:12-17). God told Noah and his three sons to multiply and fill the earth (Genesis 9:1,7), the same command given earlier to Adam and Eve. Once more, however, the time came when there was widespread disobedience and rebellion. Any lessons that had been learned from the great flood were soon forgotten. God's command was ignored.

The people settled in Shinar, located in southern Mesopotamia, in the region that would later become Babylonia. There they were determined to remain. Listen to their words of defiance: "Come, let us build ourselves a city, and a tower with its top in the heavens, and let us make a name for ourselves; otherwise we shall be scattered abroad upon the face of the whole earth" (Genesis 11:4). They deliberately refused to do what God had explicitly commanded them to do. Their words could well be translated, "I know what's best for me."

The people sought safety by congregating together, and they strove to *make a name for themselves*. The tower was a powerful symbol of their defiance and of their desire to elevate their status above that which God had assigned them. God, however, did not accept the plan they had devised. His judgment was swift and appropriate—he scattered the people throughout the earth. The lights of their city flickered and died; the tower fell into ruins. Their dreams of making a name for themselves were dashed.

We must understand that the story of the tree and the

story of the tower are the stories of *every* human being. We are not just observers. Each of us is a participant, a fellow actor in the drama. All of us have said to God in one way or another, "I know what's best for me!" We have been disobedient and rebellious. Now, a very serious question emerges that we must not try to evade.

The question is this: What has happened to the "image of God" in which we were all made? Has it perished? I do not believe so. Has it become smudged, distorted, tarnished, tattered and torn? Yes. Has it been eradicated? No. It remains clearly visible to the discerning eye of God. An ember is still present within each one of us. The possibility of it being fanned to a flame remains.

Do you and I still have worth? Is there any hope? The answer to both questions is a resounding "Yes." How can this be so? I picture myself standing back among the ruins of a tower in ancient Shinar, and looking toward a distant horizon of time and geography. Something catches my eye.

I see a shape that looks somewhat like a tree. It is not nearly as tall as the tower that once stood here in Shinar, but its top actually *does* seem to reach heaven. An intense warmth stirs within me, and I know that the hope of the entire world is brought to focus on this very special "tree"—the Cross of Jesus.

Guess Who Still Loves Us!

Honesty compels each one of us to admit the following three facts. First, "All we like sheep have gone astray; we have all turned to our own way" (Isaiah 53:6a). Second, having strayed away from God, we are lost somewhere east of Eden and are dead in "trespasses and sins" (Ephesians 2:1). The way that seemed so right to us has led to death

(Proverbs 14:12). Third, we cannot find our own way home and cannot solve our own serious problems. We must admit with the Apostle Paul, "I do not do the good I want, but the evil I do not want is what I do" (Romans 7:19). At this point, like Paul in Romans 7:24, we find ourselves crying out. "Wretched man that I am! Who will rescue me from this body of death?" There is an excellent answer to this question—one that Paul knew quite well, for he immediately went on to exclaim, "Thanks be to God through Jesus Christ our Lord!"

Agatha Christie's master detective, Hercule Poirot, once had an innocent client whom most people considered to be so obnoxious and unlikable that even Poirot found himself almost wishing that the man *were* guilty, that he *would* be hanged (James Bently, in *Mrs. McGinty's Dead*). Poirot went on to prove, however, that his client was not a murderer—just an unattractive and unlovable man.

I used to listen to a radio program called "The Shadow." Do you remember that famous crime fighter? The program always began with these eerie, chilling words: "Who knows what evil lurks in the hearts of men? The Shadow knows!" These words were followed by a peal of sinister laughter. Armed with two .45 automatic pistols, which he used with deadly accuracy, the Shadow quickly eliminated many gangsters.

Truth, however, is stranger than fiction. There is One who *does* truly know the evil that lurks in human hearts—but he does not laugh. He weeps (Hosea 11:8-9; Luke 19:41-42). This One does not try to prove our innocence because he knows that we are guilty. Nor does he use his power to destroy us.

When the people in a certain village did not welcome Jesus, two of his disciples raised this question: "Lord, do you want us to command fire to come down from heaven and consume them?" (Luke 9:54). We are told that Jesus turned and rebuked those disciples. They still had much to learn—God does not work that way.

A message that runs through the entire Bible is that God still loves those created in his image, even though they *are* guilty of disobedience, rebellion, and all kinds of corrupt practices—and are far from being easy to love from a human perspective. God, however, knew that human beings were still *worth* the ultimate price that he would pay in order that they could have the possibility of a new life. He went looking for Adam and Eve in the Garden, and he continued the search for his wayward sheep all the way to a Cross—and down to this very day.

The best-loved verse in the Bible states this miracle of love beautifully: "For God loved the world so much that he gave his only Son, so that everyone who believes in him may not die but have eternal life" (John 3:16, Today's English Version). Many of us have heard this verse so often that we may have lost some of its wonder. Let's pause right now and reflect on this marvelous truth for a while. Let its beauty capture us anew.

God's love, and the suffering it costs him, is beyond our comprehension and our ability to describe. He offers this love freely to each one of us. He knows that we are important and that we do still have worth—as incredible as that sounds! Remember, however, that freedom to make choices is part of the image of God. Yes, God's gift is offered freely—and, yes, we are free to accept or reject his gift of life. The decision we make is the most important decision we ever will or ever can make. We think, perhaps, of Eden and Shinar—and we cast *our own* ballot for life or death.

God is not, however, some sort of divine handyman. If you and I accept his priceless offer of love, he will not make just a few repairs in our life (a point C. S. Lewis stresses in *Mere Christianity*). No, God is not a handyman. He is the Creator, and he wants to make us a *new creation*. As Paul says in 2 Corinthians 5:17, "So if anyone is in Christ, there is a new creation: everything old has passed away; see, everything has become new!"

The most drastic change that can possibly occur in the life of any person is to become a new creation in Christ. When that happens to us, we are truly born again. I believe that this change is even more radical than the transformation that occurs when a Christian's physical body dies, returns to dust, and then is resurrected in a form suitable for life in heaven. None of that can happen unless we first accept God's love and become a new creation—not just repaired or patched up, but created anew.

A word of caution is now in order. Every age has had its share of "handypersons"—men and women who are only too eager to help us remodel our life, to turn us into persons of worth. Jesus foretold that "false messiahs and false prophets" would come to lead many astray (Matthew 24:24). Such persons have, indeed, come in abundance. Some mean well, but they can never provide the aid that we really need.

Various kinds of programs to help us, involving many different schemes and philosophies, are readily available. Many of these are "religious" in nature. Although some come in the guise of Christianity, the Christ known through Scripture, history, and the church is either absent or sadly distorted. In some cases, these programs might make us "feel better"—but they can *never* give us a new life.

I imagine that many of you have read *Travels With Charley*, a delightful book by John Steinbeck. Early in his long journey through the United States, Steinbeck visited a church in Vermont one Sunday morning. His account of the pastor's sermon is both amusing and instructive. Steinbeck observes that it is common "to find from our psychiatric priesthood that our sins aren't really sins at all but accidents that are set in motion by forces beyond our control. There was no such nonsense in this church." The minister assured Steinbeck and the congregation that "we didn't amount to much to start with, and due to our own tawdry efforts we had been slipping ever since."

"Tawdry efforts"—that is exactly what all of our attempts to find worth amount to unless they are centered in God's love and follow his plan to give us a new life. We cannot create a more worthy life for ourselves, but we can choose to accept the one that God offers to us. We must not ignore the overwhelming importance of this—to do so is to be fatally foolish.

I became a Christian when I was fifteen years old. Now, sixty years later, I am quite sure that Jesus meant exactly what he said—and that he was totally correct—when he told his disciples, "I am the way, and the truth, and the life. No one comes to the Father except through me" (John 14:6). Jesus is the way to a life with meaning and purpose. Jesus is the way home. He provides peace and well-being for his followers. When difficulties come, let's remember that: "God is our refuge and strength, a very present help in trouble" (Psalm 46:1). Also, Jesus said: "I will never leave you or forsake you" (Hebrews 13:5b).

The stakes are far too high for us to keep on trying to make ourselves worthy, or to rely on the guidance of "handypersons." We don't need to be repaired—we desperately need to be re-created. That is precisely what God, who loves us beyond measure, and who knows that we still have worth, is eager and able to do! Is it costly? Yes. A "new creation" costs God so much that not one of us can afford it—that is why he offers it to us as a free gift.

For a moment, let's think about things in another way. Throughout this book, we have looked at multiple ways in which persons who feel very inadequate have sought worth. None has been successful. As we have now seen, however, every person actually *already has worth*. Let's no longer ask, "How can I find worth?" Here is another question to consider: "How can a person with worth become worthless?" Is that possible? Can worth be squandered away?

A Hebrew prophet named Jeremiah has provided a very cogent and sensible answer to these questions. Sometime around 625 B. C., Jeremiah, as God's spokesman, asked the people of his time, who were following errors of the past, this question: "What wrong did your ancestors find in me that they went far from me, and went after worthless things and became worthless themselves?" (Jeremiah 2:5). About the same time, God also said, "My people have committed two evils: they have forsaken me, the fountain of living water, and dug out cisterns for themselves, cracked cisterns that can hold no water" (Jeremiah 2:13).

I am afraid that it is all too easy to become worthless—all we have to do is ignore God and rely on "cracked cisterns" of our own making. Christ is the one great treasure—compared to him all else is worthless. Paul has some wise words to share with us: "For his sake I have suffered the loss of all things, and I regard them as rubbish, in order that I may gain Christ" (Philippians 3:8b). Paul had learned to rely on the Living Water offered by Christ (John 4:10) and not on leaking cisterns.

Yes, as persons created in the image of God we do have worth. Our worth is not established by comparing ourselves with others. Our worth is not determined by what we think about ourselves, or by what other persons think about us. Our worth comes solely as God's free gift to us.

This worth, however, cannot mature apart from our continuing fellowship with the God who loves us—nor can it endure forever unless we choose to become a new creation in Christ. If we choose to separate ourselves eternally from God, then we will become totally worthless. In heaven, there is a gathering of all that is true and worthy; in hell, not even a hill of beans can grow.

I choose to make my eternal home where a Tree of Life grows, and where I can enjoy the love of my God, and worship him, the One who is pure worth, forever and ever. If you have not already done so, I hope that you will make that same choice. It is the most important choice any person can ever make.

Under New Management

As I begin writing this paragraph, I am looking at a very old Bible. More than a half-century ago, a very lovely teenage girl wrote a Scripture reference on the flyleaf, and highlighted the verse in the Bible. A few years later, the two of us met, and two years after that, we were wed. The reference that she had written in her Bible was given an important place in our life together.

The verse is Galatians 2:20, and in the old King James Version it reads like this: "I am crucified with Christ: nevertheless I live; yet not I, but Christ liveth in me: and the life which I now live in the flesh I live by the faith of the Son of God, who loved me, and gave himself for me." I like to call this my "Under New Management" verse.

The loving, triune God not only makes us a new creation, he also comes to reside with us. According to the New Testament, Christians become the temple of the Living God (2 Corinthians 6:16). The Holy Spirit dwells within us—we are under new management! What we could not do for ourselves, and what others could not do for us, God has graciously and lovingly accomplished. He has made us to be persons of worth—and he will help us live worthy lives. Let's turn now to a consideration of what that means.

CHAPTER EIGHT

Living a Worthy Life

One would expect persons created in the image of God—and therefore possessing great worth—to live worthy lives. We have seen that this is all too often not the case. For those of us, however, who have chosen to say "Yes" to God's offer to make us a new creation, who are under "new management," living a worthy life is more than an expectation—it is a solemn mandate and responsibility, and is also a genuine opportunity to experience supreme joy.

The Apostle Paul, who prayed regularly for those in Christ, included these words in his prayer for the Christian congregation in Colossae, "that you may lead lives worthy of the Lord, fully pleasing to him, as you bear fruit in every good work and as you grow in the knowledge of God" (Colossians 1:10). He wrote similar words to Christians elsewhere (Ephesians 4:1 and 1 Thessalonians 2:12).

Under Divine guidance, Paul's words became part of the New Testament and are a portion of God's message for all Christians today. We must consider these words to be more than a "hope" or a "suggestion"—they are God's direct instruction to us and they are to be obeyed. Each one of us who is a new creation in Christ should give high priority to living a worthy life. Actually, living that kind of life is something that we should *want* to do!

However, you and I who are Christians know quite well that our thoughts, words, and deeds are *not* always worthy of the Lord (as even those outside of Christ who may be watching us will probably be quick to notice). What does this mean? Are we back in Eden or Shinar all over again? What, if anything, can we do about our plight? Who *are* we, anyway?

Remembering Who We Are

We would do well to embrace and build on the amazing, glorious truth that God through Christ has declared that all of us who follow him are his *children*! The relationship we share with God is that of parent-child. The majestic, omnipotent, sovereign, and eternal God—creator of all that exists—is our *Heavenly Father*. That staggers our imagination, doesn't it? But it is wholly true—vouched for by the One who *is* Truth. We *are* the sons and daughters of God, and he loves each one of us and gives to us an abundant life (John 10:10).

I believe it is also true that each one of us is unique. Yes, we are all created in the image of God, but the One who shaped us—and continues to shape us—does not turn out exact replicas from some celestial mold, and he never produces clones. His purpose is to provide each one of us with our own unduplicated identity, thus adding a marvelous diversity, richness, and vitality to the family of God. There never has been—and never will be—anyone exactly like *you* in all of God's creation!

We are not fully grown when we enter God's family. Nearly two thousand years ago, a noted teacher by the name of Nicodemus came to Jesus one evening for a theological discussion. Jesus immediately went straight to the heart of the man's need with the assertion, "I tell you the truth, no one can see the kingdom of God unless he is born again" (John 3:3, New International Version). Similar words of Jesus are recorded elsewhere: "Truly I tell you, whoever does not receive the kingdom of God as a little child will never enter it" (Luke 18:17).

You and I are human beings who have entered this world as flesh-and-blood babies, but "flesh and blood cannot inherit the kingdom of God" (1 Corinthians 15:50). We must be born again ("born again" can also be translated "born from above") to enter God's family. Ultimately, when we enter heaven, our bodies will be transformed into a spiritual body (1 Corinthians 15:44). Thanks be to God who makes all of this possible!

We enter God's family as babes in Christ, and we must *learn* how to think and act in ways suitable for our new status. This means that we will almost certainly make mistakes that we won't even recognize as being unacceptable behavior until we have been informed of this by God, who often will teach us through the words and examples of our brothers and sisters in Christ. I believe the fictional senior devil, Screwtape, is actually correct when he says, "The Enemy wants his children to learn to walk and must therefore take away His hand; and if only the will to walk is really there He is pleased even with their stumbles" (C. S. Lewis, *The Screwtape Letters*, Chapter 8. By "Enemy," Screwtape of course means God).

Certainly, all new members of the family deserve to be instructed and guided with gentleness and kindness. No one's sins can be ignored, but harsh condemnation of our family members is not conducive to their spiritual growth—nor to ours! A key word is *encouragement.* Let us concentrate on encouraging one another as together we grow and learn—a process that I believe will continue even after we are welcomed into heaven.

On two earlier occasions in this book, I briefly mentioned persons who are mentally challenged. I have no doubt that those who cannot make reasoned choices to follow Christ—or who are limited in the extent of their ability to do so—are still persons of true worth, whom God will care for with great kindness, and in heaven all of their mental and physical infirmities will be healed. They definitely have a place in God's family. We are honored by their presence—and there is much that we can learn from them.

Henri J. M. Nouwen, now deceased, once served as pastor of the L'Arche Daybreak Community in Toronto, Canada, a community for the mentally challenged. Here are two quotations from the Epilogue of his beautiful book, *The Return of the Prodigal Son*. "The embrace of the Father became very real to me in the embraces of the mentally poor." "Handicapped people have little to lose . . . by just simply being who they are, they break through my sophisticated defenses and demand that I be as open with them as they are with me. Their handicap unveils my own." I believe we would be wise to consider these words by Nouwen very seriously. I have frequently noticed that the most profound teaching does not always come from those who hold academic degrees.

The story of the prodigal son, found in Luke 15:11-32, is probably the best-known and most-loved parable in the New Testament. When the penniless and dispirited young man finally returned home—only a shadow of the brash youngster who had left earlier with great confidence and many grand plans—his hope was that his father would be willing to accept him as one of the hired hands. When he met his father, he confessed, "I am no longer *worthy* to be called your son" (Luke 15:21b, I have added the italics).

As most of you probably know, however, the father (a symbol of our Heavenly Father) welcomed the prodigal back home with great joy and celebration. He accepted him as a *son*—not as a servant. It is crucial that you and I understand that we are sons and daughters of God—not hired hands. We have even more responsibility than a servant, but we also have the great joy of being an integral part of the family, including the opportunity to participate with God in his work. We will be wise to cultivate a correct mentality about our true status—we are God's *children*. Let's embrace that reality and, with appropriate humility, stand tall, with our head erect! Let's enjoy *working* with our Father, and also all of the *celebrations*!

Trust and Obey

"Trust and Obey" is the title of an old, popular Gospel hymn. I have joined in the singing of this song "many, many times in many, many places," and have never grown tired of its contagious blend of rhythm, melody, and words. It calls to my attention two crucial components of a worthy life—trust and obedience. Both of these must be present in good measure in a life that pleases God. And, as words in the refrain of the song remind me, "There's no other way to be happy in Jesus, but to trust and obey."

Trust! I am looking right now at the back of a dollar bill. I see words boldly printed there, "In God We Trust." I wonder how true the words really are? Does the way I earned this dollar reflect my own trust in God? Will I spend it in a manner compatible with trust in my Father?

"In God We Trust" is a nice slogan—but unless it is more than that, it is only a sham and a hollow pretense.

Trust! What does this really mean? For one thing, trust in God means that we believe what he says to us is wholly true. This just makes good sense. God *is* Truth, and he is the *only* one who actually knows truth in all of its dimensions. Other persons, willfully or unknowingly, may deceive us, and we do not always tell the truth to ourselves. To trust God means that we believe all of his words are true, and to live a worthy life we must strive to be truthful persons. If an evil voice whispers anything into our ear, we must remember that the devil "is a liar and the father of lies" (John 8:44b). We will not listen to him.

Trust in God also means that we believe he knows what is best for us—and that the best is what he desires for each one of us. We can trust him to provide all needed illumination, wisdom, and direction for every facet of our life. Because he knows us fully, we can be totally honest in his presence. We can pray with Peter Marshall, "I thank Thee that Thou dost receive me as I am—not as I pretend to be. I am so tired of pretending" (*The Prayers of Peter Marshall*). To trust God means to believe him so fully that we can quit insisting on having our own foolish way, and we can give up trying to manage our own life without Divine assistance.

To trust God also means to believe all of his promises. Sure, there will be moments of doubt, but these will give way to confidence and certainty if we continue to trust him with tenacity. None of us stands alone. We have the testimony of countless thousands of persons, extending over many, many centuries, that God does indeed keep the promises he makes to his people. Patience may be required, but the fulfillment of each of his promises is a certainty. Human beings tend to make promises rather casually—and break them even more casually. God is most definitely not like that! We can count on his promises being kept—we can trust him fully. And we who seek to live worthy lives must be scrupulous in keeping *our* promises to God, to others, and to ourselves.

When you and I affirm our trust in God, we are committing ourselves to *rely* on him. Reliance is an integral part of trust. Unfortunately, a lot of us find it easier to rely on other people—even on ourselves—than to rely on God. All too often, we find that we rely on him only as a last resort, when all else has failed. We—or at least I—need to work on this! We cannot hope to live a worthy life unless we rely on our Father in a manner that demonstrates our trust in him on a day-by-day basis and in all the dimensions of life. Only then can we truly say, "In God we trust."

Obedience! The words "obey" and "obedience" tend to make us uneasy and even fearful. They smack of legalism and suggest coercion. They raise the specter of a heavy-handed authority, and alarm us with the prospect of infringement upon our rights and freedom. However, the Ten Commandments and numerous other laws are clearly a part of Scripture and cannot be safely ignored. Jesus places the issue clearly before us with these unavoidable words, "You are my friends if you do what I command you" (John 15:14). As we have seen, you and I are free to choose—but there are compelling reasons for us to be obedient.

In most cases, children *want* to please their parents. This desire is usual and normal, but can, of course, be stifled and thwarted by uncaring or abusive mothers and dads. Fortunately, that is a problem we don't have to worry about with reference to our Heavenly Father. His love and care for us are unfailing and pure. For those of us who have become a new creation through the work of Christ, love and obedience are the expected, normal response.

Christians tend to talk a lot about God's love for them—a love that actively reaches out to all people. It is right and good that we do so. I feel, however, that perhaps additional attention needs to be focused on *our* love for God. When we stop to analyze our relationship with our Father, we may find that a deep, intense, heart-felt *love* for *him* is not very prominent—and that is a shame. Without such love, we will not be able to really enjoy his presence with us, and we will be much less inclined to give him our willing obedience. Our pursuit of a worthy life, with all of its many benefits and joys, will surely languish.

There are some Christians who, for a variety of reasons, actually are inclined to be afraid of God. Among the things that can cause such fear is an unhappy early experience with earthly parents, especially fathers, and another is a distorted and unwise emphasis on God's wrath and judgment that some Christians are exposed to in their churches. Unfortunately, there are some Christian communities that place so much emphasis on a stern, angry God that they fail to proclaim his grace, mercy, and love.

Regardless of its cause, a person cannot really love God if he or she is afraid of him. Also, fear is *not* a healthy or very effective motivation for obedience. The more we cultivate our love *for* God, the fewer problems we will have with fear. As Scripture says, "There is no fear in love, but perfect love casts out fear" (1 John 4:18a).

I believe the first reason, then, that we should obey God is that this is the normal response of a Christian who truly loves the Father. But there are other reasons. For example, we should obey because we have a God who can be trusted fully—One who knows what is best for each one of us, and who desires that we each achieve our highest potential. He wants each of us to have a happy, abundant life full of joy and peace. Doesn't it just seem obvious and reasonable that our best course of action is to follow God's instructions? After all, it is for our benefit. We may have attempted to find worth in many ways and places, but God is our sure guide to worth, and also is our Instructor in living a worthy life.

The laws that God has established for human beings to live by are *not* designed to restrict our happiness and freedom—they have been issued for just the reverse purpose. Through obedience, we are made free; through obedience, we can have true happiness. When God asks us to do something—or to refrain from doing something—we can trust his judgment. Yes, there could be times when he will request us to do that which is difficult and possibly even dangerous. Huge sacrifices may be required. We may not understand, but hopefully we will still obey because we love him and because we trust him. One day, maybe not until we are in heaven, we *will* understand and then we will say with joy, "I am *so* glad that I obeyed!"

We obey God because we love him, we obey because of the benefits that it brings to us—and we also will want to obey because obedience allows us to participate with God in his ministry to the whole world. When we stop to think about it, isn't it an amazing thing that God chooses to involve us in his work? We are his children, and despite our clumsy efforts, he definitely wants to include us in the "family business." Over time, you and I become more skillful in assisting our Father in the work of the Kingdom of God. We will never have any work as important as this.

God will never ask any of us to undertake a task without

providing us with all of the resources that we will need. He gives to all of his children both general and specific gifts and abilities—ones suitable to our own individual uniqueness, and designed to help us accomplish the work he has assigned to us. Whatever type of career we may follow, numerous opportunities will be given us to employ our gifts in our Father's work—for his enterprises pervade *all* of life. Also, let us remember to give him the glory for every success that we experience.

At this point, I would like to include some of my own words from *Long Shadows: Redeeming the Past*. "If we are Christians, persons reconciled to God through Christ, then we are also commissioned to be ministers of reconciliation (2 Corinthians 5:19). First and foremost, this means that we have an obligation to help 'prodigal sons' find their way back to their true home with God. But I believe we are also expected to help estranged persons to be reconciled to one another whenever we have the opportunity" (page 93). There are, of course, many additional ways in which we may be able to help others.

I have found that my sweetest rewards in life have not come in the form of money or applause, but rather in the looks and words of thanks from grateful persons on those occasions when I was able to help facilitate what God was seeking to do in their life. And some of my best memories are of those persons who were helpful to me in a similar way.

During his earthly life, when he was only twelve years old, Jesus asked his parents, who had been looking for him, "Do you not know that I must be engaged in my Father's business?" (Luke 2:49b, My translation). Every true child of God has the opportunity and the responsibility to participate in the business of the Father. What a grand reality! What a valid reason to be obedient! Every time that I report for work, I *know* that my life and my labor are worth far more than a hill of beans. My Employer assures me that this is true.

Trust and obedience— these are keys to living a worthy life. The tasks, however, are numerous. Let's remember that these also include the responsibility, like the one assigned to that long-ago first couple, to take care of the physical world in which we all live. Let's promote the health of our environment and be careful not to pollute and spoil the "garden." I do want to trust God. I do want to obey all of his instructions. Surely I will need help to do this. Let's look together at the resources that have been provided to enable us to accomplish our share of work in the Kingdom of God. We have indeed been called to live a worthy life and to be trusting, obedient children.

Resources for the Journey

All of us who are Christians are on a journey that began when we became a new creation in Christ. We are pilgrims. Life with God is never static. We are either moving closer to him, or the distance that separates us is increasing. Our desire should be to continue to learn and mature, and to become progressively more and more the persons he designed us to be. The journey includes much work to be done, but also many pleasures to enjoy. In the words of Fanny Crosby, contained in an old Gospel song, "Close to Thee," our prayer should be, "All along my pilgrim journey, Savior let me walk with thee."

We will need to make sure that our "religion" is real and true. At the beginning of his instructive book, *Confessions of a Religionless Christian*, Gene Owens adds an interesting postscript to an old fairy tale. He reminds us of the prince who was trapped in the body of a frog. Then one day, the frog was kissed by a beautiful princess and he was liberated. Owens suggests, however, that a female frog in the pond cried herself to sleep that night croaking, "Never fall in love with a form." Yes, indeed! We must be very sure that we are a new creation—and not just a follower of a form embodied in this or that "religion." As Christians, we have resources available only from God.

When the early disciples of Jesus became aware that he was going to leave them, in order to return to his Father in heaven, they were understandably anxious and frightened. Jesus quickly reassured them: "I will not leave you orphaned" (John 14:18a), and he added these words: "The Advocate, the Holy Spirit, whom the Father will send in my name, will teach you everything, and remind you of all that I have said to you"(John 14:26). The word "Advocate" can also be translated "Helper."

The astounding truth is this: when you and I are truly born again—and not just following the false form of a "religion"—God himself, in the person of the Holy Spirit, comes to make his permanent residence within us! In 1 Corinthians 3:16, the Apostle Paul asks this question: "Do you not know that you are God's temple and that God's Spirit dwells in you?" (See also 2 Corinthians 6:16.)

The greatest resource for our journey through life is God himself—and not some distant, far-away deity, but One who as Holy Spirit, the Divine Helper, resides *within us*. His presence is the undeniable evidence that our religion is true and not just a form and a sham. He provides comfort, instruction, wisdom, guidance, and *everything* that we need to live a worthy life—including some very important spiritual qualities that the Bible calls "fruits."

According to Scripture, "The fruit of the Spirit is love,

joy, peace, patience, generosity, faithfulness, gentleness, and self-control" (Galatians 5:22-23). The basic virtue is love—the other seven flow from it. I believe we can easily see the tremendous importance of this work of the Spirit. These eight spiritual qualities are at the very heart of worth. We cannot produce them or earn them—they are the product of God's work in our life.

You and I, however, must participate with the Spirit if these wonderful characteristics of a worthy life are to grow and mature. How can we do that? Let me offer three suggestions (additional ideas can be found on pages 141-142 of *Long Shadows*). First, prepare some cards with the names of these eight fruits written on them, and keep the cards where you will see them daily. For example, I keep such a card on a mirror in my bedroom, one in my kitchen, and also one in my car.

Second, pray daily and earnestly that God will give you the desire to have these fruits in your life, and that your heart will be fertile soil. And third, practice each of these fruits at every opportunity. The Spirit wants to do this good work in the life of each of his children. He is our greatest resource and we will want to cultivate our relationship with him—all relationships need nurture.

There are other resources available to us. These are helpful in many ways, including their role in keeping us close to our Greatest Resource. I will mention three of the most important ones. First, there is prayer. As God's children, we can talk with him anytime we wish. We will never get a busy signal or a recording machine—or a "menu." God is never away on vacation. He is always available. Since he already knows everything we are thinking and feeling we can, as noted earlier, be completely honest in his presence. On those occasions when we just don't know how to pray, the Holy Spirit will intercede for us (Romans 8:26).

When we think about prayer, our thoughts often turn first to things we would like to request for others (intercession) or for ourselves (petition). However, we will want to remember to also include prayers of praise, of thanksgiving, and of confession. Then, there are those special times when we will just want to be entirely silent and simply enjoy being in our Father's presence, with no agenda at all other than to be with him.

The last book written by C. S. Lewis is a very helpful small volume with the title, *Letters to Malcolm: Chiefly on Prayer*. Lewis reminds us, in chapter twelve, that our prayers often need to be accompanied with action on our part: "I am often, I believe, praying for others when I should be doing things for them. It's so much easier to pray for a bore than to go see him." I imagine that most of us know exactly what Lewis is talking about!

One final word about prayer. I'm afraid that some of us may feel a little like Huckleberry Finn, who said: (Miss Watson) "told me to pray every day, and whatever I asked for I would get. But it warn't so. I tried it. Once I got a fish-line, but no hooks. It warn't any good to me without hooks. I tried for the hooks three or four times, but somehow I couldn't make it work" (Mark Twain, *The Adventures of Huckleberry Finn*, chapter three). Most of us can probably sympathize with Huck!

Prayer does not connect us with any type of divine vending machine. It is true, however, that Jesus once said, "If in my name you ask me for anything, I will do it" (John 14:14). Now, what in the world does that mean? Many Christians have been puzzled and disappointed by that verse of Scripture. The key to understanding it is contained in the word "name." To ask in the "name" of Jesus means that our request will be made in accord with who Jesus is—his basic nature. Our will and desire will then be his will and desire. He can, therefore, respond in an affirmative manner. By the way, some of my most fervent prayers of thanksgiving have been those times when I looked back and was led to thank God that he had said "no" to some request of mine! Obviously, my earlier prayer of petition had *not* been made in the "name" of Jesus. But he always responds in ways that are best for his children.

Another very important resource available to help us lead a worthy life is Scripture. The Bible is the Christian's authoritative guide to faith and practice—to what we believe and how we live. We are fortunate that we now have so many good, reliable translations made from the original languages of the Bible (Hebrew, Aramaic, and Greek) into English and other modern languages. I recommend that we use at least two or three of these in our regular Bible reading and study, and that we not restrict our reading to only one version of the Scripture. Several of what I consider to be the most helpful translations have been cited at various places in this book.

The Bible comes to you and me from "long ago and far away." Some portions can be somewhat difficult to understand. We have, however, a marvelous teacher—the Holy Spirit. The Bible was written by persons who were inspired by the Spirit. He also insured that the message was preserved, and that the right books were selected for inclusion in the Bible. Now, he is immediately available to guide us in our study of the Scripture. The essential elements in God's message to us will be made clear. We should not neglect *any* portion of the Bible, but the New Testament merits special attention.

I would like to make two simple suggestions to aid you in your individual study of God's written word. First, try to enter into dialogue with what you are reading. You will find this easier to do if you underline and highlight certain portions, and if you write notes in the margins. Please don't be one of those Christians who refuse to write in their Bibles! That may sound like a pious and holy practice—but it isn't, and it limits a person's real encounter with God. Second, buy yourself a good Bible dictionary—perhaps your pastor can help you choose the one that is best for you. Of all the aids to the study of the Bible, I believe most persons will find a good dictionary the most helpful.

In addition to the Bible—our most important written resource—there is also a vast reservoir of Christian literature, both ancient and modern, that can provide us significant help in our endeavor to live a worthy life. A note of caution at this point—almost all books are expensive today and, quite frankly, some Christian literature is not worth reading and can even be harmful in some cases. I recommend that you check with your pastor, or other member of the church staff, for guidance in this matter. Some of you will also be fortunate enough to have a good church library for your use. Throughout *A Hill of Beans*, I have referred to books by Christian authors that I have found of value—perhaps you will also find these helpful.

Now, let's shift our focus. We have been concentrating on resources available to individual Christians. However, a worthy life cannot be lived in isolation; our journey is not to be made alone. As Christians, you and I are part of a vast family of God stretching through the centuries and filling our world today. It is absolutely essential that we find our place in a local church of our choice. The rewards are enormous.

Worship of God is the most important activity that we can engage in—and it is meant to be primarily a group experience (as it will be in heaven). Regular celebration of the Lord's Supper (Communion), as part of worship, is important (in my local church, we do this once a month). Private Bible study is of real value—but *group study of Scripture* can often be of even greater importance. We can and should have our individual ministries to other persons, but our church can provide additional local and worldwide *opportunities for service*. And certainly we can never thrive without the *fellowship* provided by other Christians, those with whom we can laugh and, at times, grieve. Believers in Christ encourage one another, and are very often the means used by God to communicate with individual members of his family.

We are to help and instruct one another. No group of believers is ever perfect—but *every* Christian should still definitely be a member of some local church. In no other way can we hope to live a life worthy of our Lord. One additional concern—churches *must* find ways to permit the aged and the infirm to continue to have some meaningful connection with their church.

Concluding Thoughts

Jesus, of course, never mentioned a "hill of beans." He did, however, say something quite similar. These words of his were addressed to fearful disciples: "For only a penny you can buy two sparrows, yet not one sparrow falls to the ground without your Father's consent . . . Even the hairs of your head have all been counted. So do not be afraid; you are worth much more than many sparrows!" (Matthew 10:29-31, Today's English Version.)

Yes, as ones created in the image of God, we have much worth. This has been given to us by God and not earned by our own efforts. All of the positive things we may have gained in our futile search for worth through wealth, education, fame, power, and happiness can, however, be used to help us live a worthy life.

That life begins when we become new creations in Christ. If we choose, however, to spurn God's offer to re-create us, all of our original worth will drain away—and we will be left eternally destitute and worthless. Surely, none of us wants that to happen.

To live a worthy life means that we will seek to honor God with all of our being, and to affirm that he is the only source of authentic worth. We are on a journey. Like Christian in *The Pilgrim's Progress*, our destination is the Celestial City. When we arrive, we will join our voices with countless others to sing, "Worthy is the Lamb" (Revelation 5:12). Jesus is the true measure of worth, and we will enthusiastically sing his praise!

In the language of Scripture, all Christians are called saints. I would like to conclude this book with a prayer for each reader, using the words of John: "The grace of the Lord Jesus be with all the saints. Amen" (Revelation 22:21).